BREAD AND BUTTER

BREAD AND BUTTER

BUTTER

WHAT A BUNCH OF BAKERS TAUGHT ME ABOUT BUSINESS AND HAPPINESS

Tom McMakin

ST. MARTIN'S PRESS   NEW YORK

Grateful acknowledgment is made for permission to reprint the following:

From *At Home in the World* by Stuart A. Kaufman, copyright © 1995 by Stuart A. Kaufman. Reprinted by permission of Oxford University Press.

From *Body and Soul* by Anita Roddick, copyright © 1991 by Anita Roddick. Reprinted by permission of Random House, Inc.

www.stmartins.com

Library of Congress Cataloging-in-Publication Data

McMakin, Tom.
    Bread and butter : what a bunch of bakers taught me about business and happiness / Tom McMakin.—1st ed.
      p. cm.
    ISBN 0-312-26591-3
    1. Great Harvest Bread Co.—History. 2. McMakin, Tom. 3. Bread industry—United States. 4. Businesspeople—United States. I. Title.

HD9058.B744 G74 2001
338.7'6647523'0973—dc21

                           2001019155

First Edition: June 2001

10   9   8   7   6   5   4   3   2   1

To Mary, Valerie, and Wilson

CONTENTS

INTRODUCTION

Some jobs hold you close and give you a feeling of safety, warm by your side like a long-time lover. Other jobs pick you up, shake you like a wild dog, and give you new life. In June 1993, I started working for Great Harvest Bread Co., a chain of independently owned whole-wheat bread stores whose home office is in the small town of Dillon, Montana. It rocked my world.

I came to Great Harvest looking. Looking for something to do. Looking to be part of something. Looking for a better way to be happy in this world. At Great Harvest, I found what I was looking for—and more. This is that story.

It is the tale of Laura and Pete Wakeman, founders of Great Harvest, who turned their love of great bread into a thriving business, eventually growing the business over twenty-five years into 140 stores spread across thirty-four states, each owned and run by different franchised owners, but all part of a single Great Harvest system.

This book describes that system—the store owners and the franchising company, the simple, nourishing whole-wheat bread they make, the unique way Great Harvest organizes itself in something called a freedom franchise, and the people who bake the bread and who have built the company. It is a business book. You'll find inspiration and stimulation for creating the work you really want to do and for organizing it in ways that free you and others to be your creative best.

But it is more. It is unabashedly a self-improvement book as well. If you are wondering what to do next, if your job fills your stomach but not your soul, if you wonder where the joy has gone, if you would like to learn some powerful ways to strengthen your work but also limit it so you have plenty of energy for other parts of your life, look inside this book and read the story of a decidedly not dot-com company and the people who work there. You'll learn a lot about bread and business, but you will also learn about life. I know I did.

In writing this book, I quickly realized the story of Great Harvest's business success couldn't be told without also describing how people in this system think about what constitutes a good life. Further, that this unique perspective on successful living is best told in the context of the work Great Harvesters do and the community they have built. For this reason, be prepared to see three interwoven subjects in this book: business, community, and self.

My goal throughout, however, has been to answer a single question: *How do we create health and strength in our personal lives and in the communities in which we work?*

I've discovered two less-than-obvious truths while working at Great Harvest, themes you will see surface in nearly every chapter. I've learned that the key to work and business success is to *work first on yourself.* And I have learned that the only way to create space in your life—the kind of space you need in order to grow as a person—is *to create business or work that is truly in service of your life.*

My discoveries are thanks to my relationship with Laura and Pete. They hired me and I continue to work for them, but the relationship is deeper than that. I have come to see them as mentors over the last eight years. It hasn't always been an easy partnership, but I have grown through exposure to their unique perspective on creating a successful business and a happy life. In this book you will meet them and learn what they have taught me.

I don't mean to suggest that Great Harvest is some sort of perfect community—every group has its dysfunction—just that in many ways the Great Harvest system is an example of how people can help each other lead good lives and do effective work.

For as long as I can remember, I have been on a search for some sort of integration between work, home, and spirit. Laura and Pete and all the owners at Great Harvest have taught me how to combine all three with grace and fun. It has been a revelation. If you are on this same search, I want to share with you what I have learned, much like I might pass on a particularly tasty recipe for apricot almond bread. Think of this book as a recipe for how to be happy in a confusing world. Enjoy!

Let's start by flying out to a Great Harvest Bread Co. grand opening in Indiana. You will meet new owners Terri Winn and Brian Turner, who were looking for something more in their lives—a way to express their values, love of community, and desire to make a valuable contribution in what they do. You will also get a quick sense of the business we're in. Next I'll tell you about how I came to work for Great Harvest and a bit more about myself. And then I'll introduce you to the people who started it all, Laura and Pete—how they grew the business, incorporated their strong beliefs into it, and what held their efforts together when things got tough.

Recruit the nicest, most honest, most generous and authentic people we can find—who love learning for the plain fun of it, who see business as an excuse to play, and love all of life for the sheer thrill of the bumpy ride— and bring them together in a caring community that supports these entrepreneurial types to truly *run their own thing, make their own mistakes, have their own successes, and be 100 percent themselves. That's what Great Harvest is.*

—Pete Wakeman, cofounder,
Great Harvest Bread Co.

BREAD AND BUTTER

1

DIARY OF A NEW STORE OPENING: A QUICK LOOK AT THIS THING WE DO

I'm at 35,000 feet and beginning to drop. The plane is hitting the clouds and rough air is making it difficult to keep my fingers on my laptop. I look like just another road warrior, but my clattering fingers hide a secret. I am not on my way to make a sales presentation to some great gaggle of expectant clients. I'm going to a barn-raising of sorts—helping Terri Winn and Brian Turner open their own Great Harvest Bread Co. in Lafayette, Indiana.

Terri and Brian

Terri's a fireball, maybe even a loose cannon. Meet her on a dark, starless night and you just know she'd glow. When Terri enters a room, the room's chemistry changes for the better. As buoyant as she is, you wonder whether the ropes that tether her to the ground are strong enough to hold, or whether her enthusiasm will just carry her away.

Brian is the rope that keeps Terri grounded. You get the feeling if Terri didn't originally hail from a big city, she surely must have taken to city life the day she discovered taxicabs and brightly displayed department stores. Tall and slender, Brian remains a quiet, steady country boy from Crawfordsville, Indiana. A good man, a loving father, he's the kind of person you'd want your kids to work for.

Together they make an unbelievably strong team: Terri on the front counter, talking with each customer, making them feel at home, and Brian on the oven, making sure each loaf is a gift, perfect to the point of pride.

I meet them in the bakery. Terri tells me about her background, starting with how she grew up in Franklin, Indiana. First she earned a degree as a medical technologist, then decided to become a dentist, and after a year in dental school, a pediatric dentist. Slamming through her classes and then her residency, she opened a practice in Crawfordsville. The customers just flocked in, not just for great dental care, but for Terri's attention and love.

Brian joined the Navy out of high school, rising through the ranks to become a nuclear reactor operator on one of the fleet's newest subs. Then he returned home to Indiana, back to the land of pivots and Boilermaker basketball. One of his brothers was running the family farm, so Brian went back to school, enrolling in Purdue to get a degree in business.

That's when the Brady Bunch thing happened. Terri, with three daughters from a first marriage, and Brian, with two kids of his own, fell in love at first sight. They bought a small farm in Crawfordsville and settled in.

A few months before graduation, Brian started talking about opening his own business. It had worked so well for Terri, and frankly he just couldn't see himself a cog in some larger machine—he'd already done that in the Navy. Terri suggested starting their own Great Harvest bakery. While doing her residency in Louisville, she'd patronized the store there and had grown to be a fan. And here in Crawfordsville, she noticed how many of their neighbors talked about having to travel to Indianapolis to buy bread from the Great Harvest there.

As time passed, the idea seemed like a good one, and so they applied to Great Harvest, the company that kept coming up during their dinner conversations.

Opening Day Craziness

Tim Peterson, the lead trainer for the Lafayette opening, arrives a couple days ahead to make sure the bakery is set to go. Hovering over every detail, Tim reminds me of a pit-stop boss checking out carburetor adjustments before the big race: all focused energy and attention to detail. We meet in my motel room and go over the plan: Wednesday, we'll train new employees—he in production and me on the counter. Thursday, we'll bake some bread and see who wanders in. Friday, we'll crank up to full speed with a grand opening. I am giddy, like a kid thinking about a first date. I always am at these openings. Good retail is performance art: pre-opening jitters are appropriate.

Early opening day, as the sun crawls up over the oaks and low sturdy bungalows of East Lafayette, Tim is training the dough guy. You'd think mixing the ingredients to make bread would be a simple thing, but when you get ten or twelve batches of bread going all at the same time, mixing together the flour, water, salt, yeast, and honey, it becomes a ballet of multitasking. At 6:30 the doors open and pandemonium begins. Brian and Terri get what they're after—lots of customers—but it looks like they'll be put to the test. I show up at 7:00 ready to help out at the counter but never get there. With a green crew and bread flying out the door, I spend my morning kneading dough.

At 10:00, the customers continue to come, a crowd of thirty expectant Lafayette citizens waiting hungrily for more bread to come out of the oven. In an ideal bakery, the cooling rack is the serving rack. It is in easy reach of the front counter so the counter crew can just turn around and grab the biggest, plumpest, best-designed loaf for the next customer. In this bakery, the cooling rack and the serving rack

are separated by a good fifteen feet—something we later correct. Seeing Jake, the baker, pop his loaves out on the cooling rack and seeing
those customers eyeing the distance, I remember how we literally used
to throw hot loaves across the room in our little Dillon, Montana,
bakery. I grab Lorie, one of our new kneaders, and we begin pitching
the loaves from across the bakery to the ready counter staff. The po-
tent mix of loud kinetic music, free samples of steaming hot slices
slathered with butter and honey going out to the constant customers,
and bread flying across the room gives the whole scene a pass-the-
fire-bucket quality: good honest folks baking bread as fast as we can
and getting it out to our neighbors.

By 2:00 in the afternoon, a line out the door snakes around the
newly poured sidewalk. It is the most fun I've had in a while: hot, loud,
urgent, lots of people. The freshest bread on the planet.

Why Terri and Brian Went Into Business for Themselves

That night we celebrate at the Other Bar, a publike place outside of
Lafayette. I order a pint of Harps for Brian and a Maker's Mark with
Diet Coke and two cherries for Terri. We laugh and recount the day,
so full of hope and happiness that this thing they had conceived has
been born so perfectly and full of life. Savoring our drinks, we are silly
with success and begin talking about what drew Terri and Brian to
Great Harvest in the first place.

There were several elements to their dream. They wanted to create
something that would make them proud and that earned decent
money. But they also hoped to give the gift of their efforts to this
community they so cared about. And to share something of themselves
in the process.

All of these answers come from deep within their hearts, but they
have a familiar ring to me. When people like Brian and Terri apply to

Great Harvest for a bread store, we invite them to Dillon to check us out and to give us a chance to ask them some hard questions. One of the questions we ask is, Why? Why do this thing? Why give up the security of a profession or a prosperous company to open a small business? Often the money they'll make with a store is less than what they made before. The hours can be long, the problems far from globally important. Opening a small business is not the prudent next step up the corporate ladder. Our newer owners tell stories about how colleagues and parents freak out at the news that Jane and Bill or George and Sarah are about to chuck promising careers in law or marketing to open a small whole-wheat bread store.

Interestingly, the answers we get back are remarkably similar. People want something back in their lives they feel has been taken from them. They want the freedom to design their own lives, to surround themselves with people they enjoy, to make a product (with their hands!) of which they are proud, to see their customers and know them by name, to work with their spouses, to create something in their own image, to be part of their community, to spend more time with their kids, to do less business travel, to take a shot at making some real money and to learn more about themselves. In other words, to love life—all of life—more.

I wish you could sit in on these meetings with Debbie, Mary, Mike, Mark, Maria, and me (the management team here at Great Harvest), because it is as if we have a special window on what people these days are looking for. *People want more.* Their lives are good, but they are not lives they want to lead. Last year more than 6,000 people wrote and asked us for information about opening a franchise. This interest points to a certain dis-ease with the way we work today—huddled in groups, working on specialized tasks that don't give us a tangible feeling of accomplishment, driven by company cultures that emphasize too much time spent at work and on the road, and consumed by a culture that lures us into thinking that making $50,000, $90,000, or even $140,000 a year is not enough. Frustrated, our candidates see the chance to create a different kind of life.

While the average return on investment compares favorably with other franchised businesses, the bottom line is not what draws our candidates. We don't compete (as a business opportunity) with sandwich franchises or lawn care outfits. Would-be Great Harvesters are usually thinking more radically: it's us or a homestead in Alaska—*anything to rediscover life as they dream of it.*

A couple of years back, over beers at a little family restaurant called Papa T's in Dillon, I remember talking with Mark Bruskotter from our legal department. I'll admit we were feeling no pain having spent the day skiing and having already downed our first pint of Moose Drool—but the truth of Mark's words that day still sounds right. He said, "You know what? Great Harvest is not in the business of selling a how-to-make-a-lot-of-money opportunity; it's in the business of selling a life, a better life." And it's true. People come to us looking for something different, and in that business, we have very little competition. It's as if someone said, "Let's sell freedom. There ought to be a market for that." And it turns out there is.

What a Great Crew!

The next morning we get back to work. I see that the trainer, Tim, has successfully taught Brian and Terri that bread is only half the equation. The equally important other half is creating an experience in the store that is warm and friendly but fun and bright at the same time. I decide to test their efforts. Leaving the kneading table, I slip out the back door, circle round, walk in the front door, and drink in what I see and feel. Immediately the counterperson offers me a big thick slice of still-warm honey whole wheat bread, urging me to take as much butter as I want and to take good advantage of the little honey-filled bear that sits in front of the breadboard. As the counterperson smiles at me, I notice her head gently moves to the infectious music. I count six speakers on the walls and can see why Great Harvest trainers tell new owners that music is critical to a store's success, that it is the heartbeat of the bakery. Slice in hand, I step back and take in the scene, struck by the whirlwind going on around me: four kids frenetically kneading two loaves at a time on a big butcher block table while two counter staff sweep hot loaves off a wire rack and pass them out to the customers almost as fast as they are being pulled from the oven. Behind them, the baker, a sixty-something rock of a man, stares at the huge oven in front of him, pulling out plump loaves just when they are ready. It is all there: sight, sound, smell, taste, and touch.

It is as it should be. When people walk into a Great Harvest, they should be embraced by the sights and sounds of the bakery, but at the same time, feel like they've found an oasis from their harried world.

The key, of course, to creating this warm but loose environment is the crew you hire. Yes, the building and the bread draw people in, but it is the people they meet who will bring them back. Bricks, mortar, heat, and dough all contribute, but we respond to human beings, their flesh, blood and energy. Brian's done a great job of hiring his crew, and they're all eager to learn, work, and contribute.

The Beauty of
Brian and Terri's Store

Huge barn beams stretch across the ceiling of the store. The first thing I thought when I looked up at them was, "How on earth did Brian get them up there?" Turns out he used scaffolding and a crane. The longest beam weighs more than 1600 pounds, or so said Brian. The beams all came from an old barn on Brian's mom's place. Brian and his first employee dismantled that barn over the course of three weeks, lovingly dropping the beams on the back of a flatbed truck and then resurrecting them in the store. I don't know which of Brian's relatives, now long dead, first hoisted those beams, but I know that forebearer was there to give Brian a hand the day he made them the centerpiece of his bakery. It is one of the things that makes the Lafayette store stand out. You walk in and you just know there is a story to be told.

But the star of the layout is the kneading table—front and center. Kneading tables are always celebrities in Great Harvest stores. It is here that dough, loose and unformed, gets molded and given its first hint that it will soon be bread. During the morning when we are making bread, it's to the kneading table that all eyes are drawn, as if we remember a time when most meaningful work was hammered out on big sturdy tables like this and not at a desk or on a phone.

Terri and Brian Step Back and View What They Have Wrought

It's mid-morning Saturday, nearly time for me to fly home, when I catch Brian neglecting the bread in the oven, if only for a moment. Transfixed by the crowd in his store and the line making its way out to the road, he's looking at Terri leaning over the counter talking to a customer, explaining for the thousandth time that day that she and Brian have opened this bakery because they love great bread and, oh, did she mention that the flour is fresh-ground every morning, something that no other bakery does, which is why the bread is so good? Brian's watching the hustle at the kneading table and the smile on Lori, his main kneader's face. I look at him and see her smile reflected in a tiny half-smile of his own, a small dawning of a great satisfaction becoming real. It's pride. Not a false pride, but a well-earned I-hoisted-those-beams-up-there-myself pride. I find myself humbled by the strength of his emotion.

And then I feel it myself. I'm proud to have said a few encouraging words to Terri and Brian yesterday, to have passed them a towel to mop their brow in the midst of the rush, to have coached them through what was a tough labor, and in so doing helped in some small way to bring this bakery into being. It's good work and I am glad to be here.

. . .

I t's Saturday evening and Terri and Brian have given me a final hug. I'm driving the rental car back to my motel. Breathing in cool air from the open window, I find myself wondering more deeply about why people are drawn to this idea of owning their own business, and more fundamentally, if it is possible to be an entrepreneur if one doesn't start and own a business. This is the age of the entrepreneur, after all, and its spirit is infectious. I know why Brian and Terri are in business for themselves. It is because they want to be happy. They are the sort of people who lust after what life has to give, and for them that means doing whatever it takes to get the right to call the shots. It is almost as if they don't care if they "succeed" in some standard sense of the word. For them, freedom to do it their way is all they are asking, because freedom is the ground on which a good life can be designed and constructed—beam by beam.

The Terris and Brians of the world are our heroes. Bravely they toss security to the side and stride purposefully into the breach. But what of those who work for companies or large organizations? Can they be entrepreneurs? Yes and no, I think, to myself. Yes, they can think creatively about their work and push for projects they believe in, but maybe it ends there. After all, aren't they less free to give of themselves fully, constrained by the passions and whims of their bosses?

It occurs to me that this is one of the central questions of our day, as I drive past the big Caterpillar plant. Can you be part of an institution—a teacher in a school, an engineer in a lab—and still pour your personality and spirit into what you do? Can you participate in the abundant possibilities of life with as much abandon as the true entrepreneur when you work for someone else? Really, it is a question of happiness. Do we have to be captains of our own ships to be happy?

HOMEWARD BOUND

Eight years ago my wife, Mary, and I were living in Riga, the capital of Latvia, a smallish country on the Baltic Sea that for fifty years or so was a part of the Soviet Union. It was late February and we were walking home from work. Passing the Freedom Monument, we headed east toward our little flat. Mary bought some flowers from an old woman on a side street for our coffee table at home.

As we rounded the final corner to the apartment building, we started to bicker. Our apartment was small, and I had the strong feeling that wasn't going to help us this night. The apartment was so small the bathtub was in the kitchen, which was fun most days, but tonight, promised to work against us.

Mary thought it was time to head back to the States and I didn't. We worked for the Peace Corps and were there on temporary contract, training new volunteers for their assignments. My boss had just mentioned the possibility of a permanent position for me in Kyrgyzstan—Associate Peace Corps Director in charge of the small business program there. All I had to do was help her out for another couple of months on project, then I would be promoted, which if I remember right seemed like a good deal—a step up the career ladder.

Mary, on the other hand, thought the whole offer was like the punchline to a not-so-funny joke. As we climbed the stairs to our apartment, she laughed out loud at my sudden enthusiasm for Kyrgyzstan—a place I hadn't known existed hours before. She was, to put it mildly, skeptical.

Mary's usually right when it comes to these things. Long ago I learned to trust her on the big questions. Which is why a month later we were wheeling our Jeep Cherokee off of I-90 onto the Orange Street exit into Missoula, wondering what exactly had prompted us to move to Montana.

Not that we hadn't gotten good at answering that question. It seemed like everyone from our parents to the fellow at the storage shed where we'd kept our things while we lived overseas had asked us. I can still remember what we'd tell people, "Wherever we have worked, we have liked what we did. And there have always been opportunities, someone saying, 'Come, take this next step,' but despite this, we always found ourselves thinking, 'That's great, but this isn't where we want to live for the next ten years.' So this time we are going to move first to a place where we'd like to live and then figure out what we are going to do when we get there. We've always wanted to live in Montana. So that's where we're going."

Which sounds good and brave, but once we were here, driving down Higgins Street in a town in which we'd previously spent but a day, trying to find Lambros Realty and the apartment they had listed in the morning paper, we careened from feeling elated to being scared witless. The official answer suddenly sounded glib. After all, what *were* we going to do?

A Bit of Luck

All of which made my discovery some two months later that much more special. I ran into our little ground-floor apartment practically bursting. "I've found it!" I yelled, giving Mary a hug. "There's this great little bread company located in a small town three hours south of here. And they're looking for two people. It's perfect."

At least the job announcement made it sound ideal. The company, Great Harvest Bread Co., was looking for a newsletter editor and bakery traveler, their operations being spread out across the country. They also wanted a legal coordinator. While I had never edited a newsletter before, I was confident I could make it sound like I could do the work. And Mary had actually worked for a law firm before, so that seemed right. But it wasn't the jobs themselves that got me so excited, it was the way the ad talked about what the company did and how they did it. Little things like "four weeks vacation by the third year, generous profit sharing, and a 40-hour maximum work week." I'd never heard of a company that bragged that it went home at 5:00, but I liked it.

I sat down on the floor and read Mary the ad.

"Great Harvest is a franchise of specialty whole-wheat bakeries which are located mainly in large cities in thirty-five states. Dillon is home to the franchise headquarters. . . . People who do well at Great Harvest love great bread, are super nice, and have a full personal life as important to them as their work. . . ."

That sounded like us.

Then there was their mission statement:

> Be loose and have fun,
> Bake phenomenal bread,
> Run fast to help customers,
> Create strong, exciting bakeries,
> And give generously to others.

I called the franchise the next day to talk about the position and ended up speaking with Bonnie Harry, a bakery field representative.

"What's up with all this talk about a full personal life?" I asked Bonnie.

Bonnie explained, "One of the most important things for us is

balance. We figure, why live in Montana and not have time to enjoy it?"

Indeed.

Great Harvest

We got the jobs. From the start I felt like I had been admitted into
some kind of elect society. I remember Dana Tornabene, the HR
person at the time, telling me that there had been more than 400
qualified applicants for the position for which I had been hired. She
said it seriously, and in a way that left me with the feeling that I was
both really good and really lucky. She then set out some expectations
for my first couple of weeks. Read every newsletter that had ever been
written at Great Harvest; learn how to bake bread and, in general, how
to run a bakery; memorize the names of every person in the system—
about 140 names in all. She warned there would be a quiz.

Dana's schoolmarmish care was counterbalanced by the enthusiasm of Hans, Mark, Janet, and Bonnie, my department-mates in Field
Services. Each of them pulled me aside that first week and told me
not to worry too much, that the first step was to "get the Great Harvest
culture." After that, I would have "tons of freedom to make up your
job as you see fit."

I set about my studies and soon had a list of questions that filled a
legal pad:

- Where are the founders, Laura and Pete Wakeman? They
  run the place and I only saw them once when they hired me,
  which seems weird for a company that only has twenty people
  in its office.
- Why all this close attention to timecards for positions that seem
  to be the kind that would be salaried in other companies?
- What kind of franchise is this anyway? I thought franchises
  were about slavish consistency between stores, yet all I read

about is how owners of Great Harvest Bread Co.s are free to
do whatever they want. What's the point?

- Why does this bread taste so good? Why is it so different
  from whole-wheat bread I've ever tasted before?
- What is the "learning community" that everyone keeps talking about?
- How do these bread companies stay in business, giving away
  as much bread as they do? How can the rule that every customer gets a big free slice of bread make any sense?
- Why do people in this group seem happy most days? What's
  the secret?

I'd learn the answers to some of these questions quickly, everyone
was so willing to explain how things worked at Great Harvest. But
answers to other questions would take time. A community's values
can be easily described, but often don't make sense until those values
are experienced—a process that for me involved making mistakes and
learning their importance on my own.

.   .   .

My enthusiasm for Great Harvest in those first months knew no
bounds. Summer that year was full of hikes to high mountain
lakes, new furniture, and wide-eyed wonder at how lucky we were.

It wouldn't always be like this. Later, I'd have some pretty low
moments as I lost my way.

But for now I was close to euphoric. Here's a letter I wrote to an
old friend, Barry Vesser, who is now the executive director of a community development corporation in rural California:

Barry,

I always told you I was a saint in my last life. Now I have
proof. Karma has knocked at my door and is delivering the
goods. My new job is great. It feels like I am playing hooky
from the life of misery I should be leading. It is as if I were

skiing, and after a really nice stop, the kind that has you spraying snow all over, I look down and see a wonderful gold nugget—heavy and rough but bright like a hot ember. I pick it up and can't believe my luck. I mean, no one has the right to find money when they are skiing. It is just too good. Well, I've moved to Montana and gotten myself a job with the most amazing company, so karma it must be.

The people are unbelievably nice. The bread is great, the community full of solid purpose. And Dillon. . . . Imagine making real money and living in this place. I look out my office window and see the mountains. We are nearly completely surrounded by public lands and vast cattle ranches. There are cross-country ski trails everywhere and even a little downhill place 45 minutes away. And talk about being isolated. You know how I like being far away from things. I'm an hour from the nearest Wal-Mart! In America, it doesn't get any more rural than that.

I can't imagine a better fit for me. I get to do work I love—helping people start and run small businesses—in a place I really dig.

Stay tuned. Sometimes, it seems almost too perfect. I'm half expecting to learn that a bunch of former employees are buried in the basement like in *The Firm*.

Tom

I still work for Great Harvest—and I still love the place like a pair of old boots. But—no question—we've covered some miles together.

Mary and I are different people now. We bought a house in town. We have a little girl, Valerie, and a son, Wilson. Great Harvest is more than twice as big as when we started. And now instead of being the newsletter editor, I am the chief operating officer of the company and Mary heads our legal department.

But there's a lot more to this story and to those eight years than just the acquisition of a house or the birth of our children. And it starts with Laura and Pete Wakeman, cofounders of Great Harvest.

3  THE RIGHT STUFF

It's mid-winter in 2000. Eight inches of new snow covers Dillon. It looks beautiful, like someone has smoothed a layer of white icing on the town—spoonfuls on the feed bins and $500 pickups in the used car lot, a couple of healthy dollops on the old Safeway building, and a few more on the Burlington Northern locomotives parked behind the depot.

I love the snow in the West—it's so light and cold, gone in a puff with the first hint of a wind. The Mid-Atlantic snow I grew up with is heavy and sodden. As a kid, I remember coming home frozen from an afternoon sledding and having my jeans soaked. We'd put plastic bags in our boots and big garbage bags in the seats of our pants between the long underwear and the jeans, but nothing helped. This snow is different, the way snow ought to be—airy and full of volume like a fine down comforter draped over everything, insulating us from our worries.

Cofounders

It's a little before seven on a Friday evening. In preparation for writing this book, I've asked Laura and Pete Wakeman to meet me at Papa T's for beers and a few questions. I'm interested in the twenty-five-year history of Great Harvest, but more, I am interested in who they are.

I remember the first day I met Laura and Pete outside of the hiring process. It was at a company meeting in September of my first year with Great Harvest. They had been gone all summer, having taken three months off to camp and hike with their daughters. The pulse of the office quickened in anticipation of their return. It was clear they were a kind of life-force in the business, and people were looking forward to seeing them. I was a little daunted, to be honest. After having read the old newsletters, as Dana had assigned earlier in the summer, many written by Laura and Pete, the pair seemed larger than life. Both are quiet sorts, and that quietness can give them an air of inscrutability when seen from a distance. In person, however, I got a strong feeling that they were approachable, open, friendly, and transparent, eager to tell stories and hear yours.

I'd had lots of conversations with the two of them over the years. Still, this evening at Papa T's would be a treat, a rare chance to ask some of my hardest questions. I was interested in what made them tick. That's because in some ways their story is the story of Great Harvest. While they are not the whole company—in fact, Pete would be the first to tell you, "We're just two people, Laura and I. This company is a whole lot bigger than we are"—they are to Great Harvest what an acorn is to a mighty oak. They invented the bread. The first store that opened in Great Falls was theirs. It was their idea to build the company into a franchise, and their strong beliefs both ground and lift the company. The way they think—which is a little different from the way most people think—operates as a kind of genetic code for the organization as a whole.

They walk through the heavy metal front door of Papa T's and unbundle from the cold. Laura looks around the room, spots me, and gives me a wide smile and a little hello. Pete, stomping the snow from his feet, follows. They run or bike every day, even through the winter, and as a result their faces have the windburnt look of North Sea fishing captains. I see them and am struck all over again by their complete lack of pretense. Their smiles are open and real. They greet me without a trace of self-consciousness or affectation.

In Love

I start at the beginning: "How did you meet?" To most of us who know them, they seem indivisible.

"We lived in this small town in central Connecticut called Durham," says Pete. "I had a friend from Boston who was a city kid. Belonged to a gang and everything. He came down to Durham to visit. I was a country kid, but we were best friends. One day during a snowball fight, we started throwing snowballs at Laura and her friend, and he said to me, 'Who's that?' and I said, 'That's the most beautiful girl in Durham High.' The minute it came out of my mouth I went, 'What's that?' It was a weird thing to say because it was just Laura, who'd been my sister's friend since seventh grade. But it was as if a lightbulb went off in my head and after that . . ."

"It must have gone off in my head too," says Laura, "because I remember going to a party, and I just walked over and asked you why you had never kissed me. Which was definitely not something I would have ever done normally."

"Then, my senior year," remembers Pete, "I left to finish high school at a place called Deep Springs in the deserts of California. . . ."

Laura nods, picking up the story. "He goes off to Deep Springs, and I remember thinking, 'Well, that was fun but I'll never see him again, because everyone always tells you that when you're a kid.' But then we wrote each other every day for two years."

Pete nods his head. "It is hard to imagine, but that's 700 letters times two—1,400 letters. We *never* missed a day."

I look at them and know it's true. Sometimes Mary and I will get to talking about things like this, and we both agree that Laura and Pete are still more in love than most couples we know. It is one of the reasons, I'm sure, there are so many couples in Great Harvest. A husband will be good at the front counter and marketing, and a wife will love making the bread and maybe creating the back office systems (or the other way around). And together, they are stronger than they would be apart. Laura and Pete work together that way. Pete is our inventor, chief business strategist, and resident philosopher, while Laura rides herd on hiring, managing the day-to-day stuff, and tracking the numbers. Together, they make our little company in Dillon as strong as it is. I know, seeing them in action, that creating a strong team is the first step to starting an effective business.

Uncommonly Good Bread

I wonder how they started in the baking business. "I baked bread as a kid," says Pete. "I remember the first loaves I made were with my Aunt Polly, something called Anadama bread, a kind of cornmeal-molasses blend. Later at Deep Springs I became the school's resident baker. This was the late sixties, and I can remember when the *Whole Earth Catalog* came out. We devoured each issue, eventually scraping together the money to order the *Tassajara Bread Book*. I did a lot of experimenting. I remember baking one loaf so hard that my friends built it into a stone wall. A friend of mine wrote recently that it finally fell out of the wall. Right from the start, however, I loved baking."

When it came time to head off for college, Laura and Pete both picked Cornell, and according to Pete, the idea of bread followed them to Ithaca. Pete remembers, "My sophomore year, I waited too long to find a summer job and suddenly found myself looking for work. When I couldn't find anything, I began baking whole-wheat bread and sold it by the side of the road. Our family's house was set back from a small road that led to the beach. I set up a card table, made a sign that said 'Homemade Bread,' baked loaves out in our barn, and sold them to people headed to the beach. I did all right. The next summer Laura joined me, helping me expand operations. We called it 'The Happy Oven.' "

Laura adds, "I tasted Pete's bread, and it was uncommonly good. I had been raised on white bread. But this was really different. I was working at the hospital at the time, but baking bread and selling it with Pete seemed like a lot more fun. Pete could sell whatever he made, so we decided to make a real project of it."

I find this early relationship with bread and business quite remarkable. One of the most important questions people ask themselves these days is—"What should I do with my life?" Many of my friends want to start their own businesses, but none of them seem to know what business to start. "I don't know what I'm good at," they say.

People follow one of two paths in "making" their lives. One is to wander through, making choices and letting those choices add up to a life direction. The other is to recognize that they have an innate gift to give the world, and that life and work satisfaction is a question of how closely they listen to and follow that inner call. Laura and Pete's lives definitely followed this second path. While other kids were saving money to buy their first car or take a trip to Mexico, Laura and Pete were perfecting their recipe and asking themselves whether dry or compressed yeast made better whole-wheat bread. I think about myself, and I'd have to say I've been more of a wanderer throughout life. Clues about my life's work were not lying about the playpen. This first path has added up to a good life for me, one filled with energy and purpose, but I have a feeling it also explains why I am not an entrepreneur and why Laura and Pete are. A single, early focus in life is the ground from which many entrepreneurs spring.

Pete's dad had a strong personality—he was an industrial designer and then an independent inventor. Laura grew up poor, had to earn her own money early in life, and learned to watch pennies from the start. As much as their knowledge of their innate gifts seemed to lead them, these powerful family influences also set the stage for their later success. This squares with research on successful entrepreneurs, a majority of whom are the offspring of independently minded parents.

Heading West

A year older than Laura, Pete graduated first with a degree in Agricultural Economics. "I really wanted to farm. I'd been working on a dairy farm, helping out with the milking in the morning, and I thought that'd be just right. As soon as Laura graduated, we decided we would go to Iowa or Minnesota or Wisconsin. I just loved those farms. I still do. I was telling our daughter Addie this story just a couple of weeks ago. She was trying to figure out what she was going to do—you know, when you're in college, you're trying to pick a path and focus on something—and I was telling her it doesn't matter. Any goal, really, any *strong goal* will do the trick, because when you pick a goal, you're identifying a few things you care about. In that goal to be a farmer, there were the two big things we cared about. One was to be in a rural area and the other was to work for ourselves. Even in those days, there was flat no way I was going to work for somebody else." Before chasing their dream of farming, however, the two headed west and took a vacation, backpacking across Montana between Yellowstone and Glacier National Parks.

"It was a great trip," remembers Laura. "It was just us in those mountains. We loved it. One day, we stumbled on a bunch of wheat farmers who had flown into Shaeffer Meadows, which is the only airstrip grandfathered in the middle of the Bob Marshall Wilderness Area. I remember they had ice-cold beer—right there in the middle of the wilderness. It was a quasireligious experience. . . . It was just so right. We knew right then that we wanted to figure out a way to be wheat farmers!

"You know," she continues, "a lot of people think we woke up one day and thought 'Let's be entrepreneurs.' It wasn't that way. We were in our twenties and out in Montana. We just thought, 'Let's figure out a way to stay out here.' "

Pete agrees. "All we wanted to do was stay in Montana and have time to hike and enough money to buy sleeping bags. That's what drove the whole thing. The idea from the beginning was to run this business so we could lead our lives. If you allow your life to interweave itself in your business to the point where you can't do what you feel like doing when you want to, what's the point? You do a business like this so you can have fun with your life."

I sit there, look across the table at the two of them, and smile to myself. People wonder where it came from—this balance in their lives—but I can see now it was all right there from the start. Laura and Pete started a bread business so they could lead good lives.

Business in Service of Our Lives

I remember my first few months working at Great Harvest. Hans, Mark, Bonnie, and Janet—my new cohorts in the Field Services department—would tell me over coffee at Anna's Restaurant that they believed baking bread and opening bakeries was about helping other people, but also about making good lives for themselves. "At Great Harvest," they said, "our lives are not in service of this business. *This business is in service of our lives.*"

It is a perspective that continues to pervade the company's culture. We do the work because it gives time and money to do the things we like.

This is one of the first lessons that Great Harvest has to teach: Our businesses and our work should not be means to distant ends. They should make us happy right now. If we wake up one day and find ourselves working for the business, as opposed to the business working for us, it is a clue that things are dreadfully out of whack.

I think of Bonnie, my first friend at Great Harvest, and now one of the system's most senior field people. Talk to her and she'll tell you she works at Great Harvest because her job allows her to travel, meet new people, help them grab hold of dreams, and at the end of the day have plenty of time left over to ski Maverick Mountain or Big Sky. Working for Great Harvest is as freeing to her as owning her own business. On a break once in my early days at Great Harvest, Bonnie put it to me straight. "I say, 'Keep doing this thing as long as it's fun. *Not one minute longer.*' "

Which is a heresy of sorts. It challenges the way a lot of people think these days, or at least that's what I keep reading in the popular press. There, the near-constant theme is, "Work like an insane person, go public, and cash out."

Great Harvest, I learned quickly, is built on a very different proposition—the idea that we ought *not* to build institutions whose purpose is to give us a good life, only to wake up one day to discover we have given birth to great monsters intent on destroying our lives.

The First Bakery and the Forty-Hour Rule

After that first summer hiking, Laura and Pete settled in Great Falls, in north-central Montana. Pete took a job on a wheat farm, helping with the harvest. Laura worked in the school system as a nutritionist. Later, when the wheat crop was in, Pete tried to get an agricultural lending job in a local bank, figuring that by being close to deals, he would eventually be able to buy a farm and get into wheat farming. While interviewing, though, one kind banker said, "Kid, a degree from an Eastern Ag school really won't cut it here. What you are is a baker. Check out the Sugar and Spice on First Avenue. It's bankrupt: maybe you can work something out." This was all the invitation Pete needed to be his own boss. He rented the building, spent $200 on painting, and opened the first Great Harvest in June 1976.

The little bakery was a hit. In short order Laura quit her job and joined Pete. Customers responded. Remembers Laura, "Great Falls is a big farming town with an Air Force base and we were a little worried about being thought of as a hippy bakery. . . . Whereas in Connecticut we used to dance around in our bare feet while we made the bread, here we dressed up and went for a neat image. But we needn't have worried so much. People just loved the bread."

To this day people find the bread strangely magnetic. Made with the simplest of ingredients—whole-wheat flour, water, salt, yeast, and something sweet like honey or molasses—the bread isn't like the hard-crusted white breads that have taken off in the last ten years. It is simpler fare. And it's really good—salty and sweet at the same time, and full of whole-wheat taste. As Terri Winn told her customers, much of the flavor comes from the fact that Great Harvest owners fresh-grind their wheat in the back of the stores every morning. It turns out that fresh-ground wheat, like fresh-ground coffee, has double the flavor of flour that has been sitting around in a warehouse for weeks or even months. From the start, Laura and Pete's commitment to making a unique and an especially good product was the foundation on which their success was built.

Laura and Pete took an apartment in the old Dearborn building on 5th Street around the corner from the bakery. "We'd regularly go out drinking and dancing with our friends," remembers Pete, "stay up all night, and then hit the bakery in the morning. It was fun. But, you know, we always tried to keep the business from running over our lives. Even then we had the forty-hour rule for ourselves."

One of the most unusual things I found when I joined Great Harvest is this so-called forty-hour rule. No one at the Great Harvest main office in Montana is allowed to work more than forty hours in a week. The time cards I noticed my first days at work are to make sure we stay on track, even though we are all salaried.

Why the rule? Because if you don't watch out, people will start working fifty and sixty hours in an effort to do a good job, and pretty soon everyone will think they need to work that hard lest they be thought of as the office slacker. Suddenly the culture in your little office shifts and everyone is allowing the business to take over their lives.

That and people who work forty hours are kinder, more thoughtful, and more effective coworkers. In the Dillon office, that's important. We're in the people business. Our day-to-day customers are the owners of our stores. When they call, we need to be in a positive, open, gentle space. We are teachers and problem-solvers by trade, and when we're not rested and recharged, we don't do our job well.

Adds Debbie Harrison Huber, our head of training and store support, "I work forty hours a week, which is very different from a lot of my friends. But their days are filled with emails, nonwork phone calls, and other things that don't have to do strictly with work. We are here eight hours a day, but we are expected to work one hundred percent on Great Harvest. We spend a little less time at work, but it's more concentrated."

To be clear, the employees who work for the franchise office partially pay for this privilege. I've run into envious executives who sneer the forty-hour perk will evaporate the day the bloom is off freshly baked bread. They see the forty-hour culture as a benefit that only a rich company could afford. But they are wrong. When figuring our pay ranges, we deliberately benchmark positions in our company to national averages and then make a forty-hour deduction. It goes like this: If you are a receptionist working for the franchise, no deduction is calculated. That's because receptionists working for other companies with which we compare are not expected to work hours above and beyond their straight forty. But as you move up the pay scale, say to the position of a field representative, we figure if you were working for another company, you'd be expected to work "extra" hours in your effort to "do what it takes to get the job done." By the time you get to my position, that expectation can be considerable. Senior executives in many companies log long hours—sixty and seventy hours a week are the norm with surges to the one hundred plus range not unusual. Therefore, because I am both expected and required to work only

forty hours in a week, my pay range is calculated by researching what
other chief operating officers make in similar-sized companies and
then splitting the difference between the hourly wage I'd make if I
took a salary and worked forty hours in a week and the hourly wage
I'd make if I worked seventy hours in a week to adjust for the radical
difference in hours I work in comparison with others who do similar
work.

The result of this calculation is that we can afford to hire more
people to do the work of Great Harvest than can other companies our
size. Each of these people works for a little less time. This is good for
all of us at Great Harvest, because we get to go home at 5:00 and
build snowmen with our kids while it's still light. But it is also good
for the company, because as it turns out the first forty hours of a
working person's week are much more productive than the second
forty.

It is also beneficial for the company because we are able to attract
top quality people. Competition among firms for the best talent is keen
these days, but that's not the case at Great Harvest. Recently, we
advertised for a couple of field rep positions and were overwhelmed
by the response: 500 good applications for two jobs. Why all the interest? Because after a certain point, lots of good people don't want
more money, they want a better life. It turns out that Great Harvest
is one of the few companies out there offering the time-and-lifestyle-
plus-not-quite-as-much-cash package. And there are a lot of buyers.

Finally, the forty-hour rule is good for the town of Dillon, because
it frees up intelligent and enthusiastic people to spend time on civic
projects if they choose. I think of Lee Christianson, for example. By
day Lee's our senior trainer, but by night he's a prime mover in the
local Lutheran Church. Or I think of Kathy Peterson's involvement
with medical causes; or Maria Emmer-Annes' work with the Arts
Council; or Mary's support of the Women's Resource Center. Involvement such as this is the lifeblood of a small, rural community like
ours. If business really is in service of our lives, it makes sense that we

have time to support the community in which our lives and our businesses unfold.

·   ·   ·

Whenever I tell the story of Laura and Pete's beginnings, I see a young couple in love with each other and with life. It is a picture of a good, happy life. It makes me vaguely envious. I want what they have. I want to be happy.

But what is happiness?

I remember thinking about this question one day while driving past Clark Canyon Reservoir, all frozen and bleak, and figured I'd pull together a rough definition of happiness and see how it felt.

Happiness is making progress on who we really want to be, growing toward our more perfect self. I figure Captain Meriwether Lewis was happy that day in the summer of 1805 when he walked through this small valley. He was happy because he saw himself as America's ears and eyes as he made his way overland to the Pacific Ocean. He was happy because, after repeatedly being thwarted by the immensity of the Rocky Mountain front, his guide Sacajawea recognized the Beaverhead Valley as the place she had been born. Happy because she was able to lead him to Camaweait, her brother, and to horses and a relatively low spot across the Bitterroot spine. Happy because he was moving toward being who he thought he was meant to be: discoverer of a nation.

That's the way it is with me. Happiness is not about owning my own home or making a certain amount of cash; it is about making good progress toward my ideal self. Each day is a fresh opportunity, a chance to learn from the last day and do a little bit better. Happiness is not measured in things or even relationships. It is the rush I feel when I get off the dime and start heading in a good new way.

Pete said to me the other day, "Happiness has something to do with adaptation. There's a feeling you get when you are perfectly adapted that is more than comfort, it's a surge of real happiness. I would be very unhappy swimming in ice salt water at twenty below zero, but a polar bear is perfectly adapted to that. He must feel that playful surge of happiness on certain perfect days, when the sun and the water are just right, and he slips beneath the ice with powerful strokes after a perfect fat seal, perfectly adapted. We people get that same surge of happiness from a job well done, from being the best at something, or just from a perfect day well lived—not perfect for a polar bear, but perfect for us, because we are perfectly adapted. Happiness is growth, and growth and adaptation are related by a simple equation: growth equals increasing adaptation."

Which makes sense to me. My ideal self—that little vision I carry around with me in my head of who I want to be—is really a picture of me fully adapted, a polar bear diving and turning in the ice water, happy, with a wide smile on my furry face.

4

GUIDING VALUES

In early 1978 people started coming to that first bakery and asking Laura and Pete to help them open their own little whole-wheat bakeries. Laura and Pete thought, "Why not?" It seemed like a relatively painless way to supplement their income. The first store they helped open was across the mountains in Kalispell. The second was in Billings. Soon after, they started thinking about franchising in an organized way. From the start, they thought of franchising not as a way to open lots of bakeries, but as a way to help people lead good lives. "That was the whole thing for us," says Pete. "We just wanted to give people the chance to lead the kind of life we had." They say entrepreneurs are often not motivated by money but, instead, feel they are on a crusade. This was the case with Laura and Pete.

In 1982, they sold the Great Falls store to Pete Rysted, who moved from Minneapolis to buy the bakery. That freed them up to move to Dillon and make their living from franchising alone. Remembers Laura, "We decided if we could make $12,000 a year from the franchise, we could live on that. What we really wanted was more free time."

As businesses grow, they have a way of revealing the deeply held values of their founders. For Laura and Pete, these ranged from a commitment to run a business with no debt to a love of living in rural Montana.

No Debt

Pete Rysted, who stills owns the bakery in Great Falls, is a mountain climber. This explains his sturdy legs and barrel chest set on a slight frame. Having baked for eighteen years, he is a Great Harvest original, stubborn about bread quality and committed to living a simple life, which for him means plenty of exercise and time with his wife Mel and his youngest son Jake. It also means living modestly with a minimum amount of debt. Remembers Pete, "I learned so much from Laura and Pete, and not just about baking, but about life. For example, I loved how simply they lived. Laura and Pete always paid cash for everything. If they didn't have the cash, they pulled back on what they were going to buy. They still do that. It sounds like common sense, but in my experience, it is really rare. I remember when the two of them bought this tiny house in Great Falls, actually in Floweree, a little town north of Great Falls. The house and ten acres cost $5,000. It sat in the middle of a field. For three years, there wasn't any plumbing and definitely no phone. The two of them lived that way because that's the money the bakery was making then. I am sure they could have taken on a mortgage and gotten a bigger place, but they didn't. Laura and Pete have never believed in debt. I've always admired them for that."

Unsurprisingly, Great Harvest Franchising is privately held and owes no major money to banks, venture capitalists, or stock-holding equity partners. This gives us the freedom to run the business by our own rules. The same is true of Great Harvest bakery owners. One of the things people discover if they head down the path toward possibly owning a franchise is that we require them to have most of the money they need to open a bakery up front. That keeps our owners out of big-time debt and focused on using the bakery to create a good life for themselves and their family.

The idea that you shouldn't use "other people's money" to build a business (or a life) is foreign to most of us. We live in a time that says, "Borrow big, cash out early." Talk to a venture capitalist and the first thing they want to know—after your idea—is your "exit strategy," by which they mean how are you going to sell this thing so they can get their cash and profits out. As a culture, we have lost the idea that we might create a business meant to last, whose primary purpose is to be part of our lives.

The lesson of Great Harvest is that there is another no-debt way to start a business successfully. Not taking on debt means sacrificing good things—you can't grow as quickly, for example. All of our growth has been self-financed, meaning that we grow as much as our profit for the previous year allows.

Anyone who has been part of a fast-growing concern knows how cash flow has a habit of tripping you up. Your business makes money, putting, say, twenty percent to the bottom line. Things are good and new orders start coming in. The company accepts the orders, promising to deliver by a certain time. In order to deliver, the company must purchase new supplies and maybe even rent larger space and hire more people. To pay for this, the company uses profits from the previous year, which is fine unless your new orders are too big, in which case your cash on hand is insufficient. This is the moment of truth for many businesses. You have three choices. You can call your clients and say, "Sorry, we can't handle your business," you can seek debt financing, or you can sell part of your company to raise the necessary cash to cover the costs of growing your business. Rapid growth or freedom. That's the trade-off. At Great Harvest, we've always chosen freedom.

Live in a Place You Love

After Laura and Pete sold the bakery to Pete Rysted, they moved from Floweree to Dillon, three hours south. Pete Rysted remembers: "They told me, 'As long as we are in Great Falls, people will always think of this place as our bakery. They need to think of it as your place.' "

Adds Pete Wakeman, "We moved to Dillon because we liked it so much—it seemed so real. It wasn't a touristy town like Bozeman or Helena. It was all feed bins and dogs in the backs of pickup trucks, and for us that was really attractive."

This realness continues to be one of the big reasons most of us in the home office live in Montana. Over the years, some have suggested we move the franchise to a more central place like Denver or Chicago. And I have to admit there are days, flying into Idaho Falls at night and faced with a two-hour drive north, when I know exactly what they're talking about. But it won't happen. We like living in Montana too much. You should enjoy the place you live. For me it doesn't get any better than seeing my five-year-old wading naked in the Big Hole River, pointing at a herd of five whitetail does feeding quietly two hundred yards away.

It isn't necessarily Montana, though. It is that you have made a choice to be in a place to which you are drawn. You can like a place for all kinds of reasons. Or *not* like it. Mary and I meet people here in Dillon all the time who are aching to leave. Most of these folks grew up here, never having made it to somewhere else. They feel trapped. The ones who are happiest have made the choice to be here, like Mike Basile—he's our chief financial officer. He grew up in Bozeman, but made the move to the coast right out of school to work for a big accounting firm in Portland and then for a bio-tech startup before coming back to Montana. Now he's psyched to be back, near his folks and close to the outdoors he grew up with.

Sustainable Growth

As Great Harvest grew, Laura and Pete hired a small staff to help out and then bought a building on Idaho Street. Their focus now was on this new business of teaching people how to build and run whole-wheat bread stores. There were bakeries in Missoula, Bellingham, Spokane, and—in a big move because it was so far away—Kansas City. Growth was steady and has continued to be strong over the years. At Great Harvest, we like growth because it is fun—it keeps us alive and the challenges fresh. As fun as it is, though, we try not to become obsessed with it. Growth is good, but it's not the only goal.

In fact, we consciously limit our growth—something you don't hear much about these days. Even though we had slightly in excess of 6,000 inquiries into our franchise opportunity last year and nearly 1,000 *bona fide* applications for new stores, we opened just fifteen bakeries. The fact is we've never grown at a rate in excess of thirty percent in a year and tend to average a much more comfortable ten to twenty percent.

All this means we will not be the next coast-to-coast phenomenon à la Starbucks. Neither will we be the next "sure-thing" public offering. We will continue to grow, to be sure. We just won't be doubling in size in a single year. This has real consequences for us. It means, for one thing, that none of us will make a ton of money doing Great Harvest. That's a go-public-sacrifice-your-life thing, which is not for us.

Slow growth certainly has it advantages, though.

For one thing, it is sustainable. We all know stories of friends in startups: the all-nighters, the kids who get used to not having Mommy or Daddy come home until they're in bed, the endless stream of broken promises to spouses. By capping our growth, Great Harvest has avoided a lot of that pain. Says Bonnie Harry, "It all gets back to why you are in the business. For us, it is to have a life worth living. We try not to lose sight of that. We see ourselves doing this for a long time to come."

By not borrowing money, we are not in bed with people whose values differ from our own. When you decide to grow at a rate faster than your revenues can support, you end up hooking your wagon to a banker, an angel investor, a venture capitalist, an investment bank, or the equity markets. This new partnership—while seemingly harmless or even a sign of your success—ends up turning you into a commodity, which isn't always a great thing. All your lofty goals about creating a balanced workplace become just words. That's because your investors don't care about your lifestyle or whether the business you are running is supporting you in the life you want to live. They are concerned about one thing. That's return on investment. This goes up the harder you work and down the less you work.

The choice between control and fast growth is one of the more dramatic moments in business. The spirit of Faust swoops in and circles around you as you decide what to do: grab the short-term cash and grow quickly, or refuse the money and keep control of your life. The world of finance is full of big words and byzantine concepts, but for all its dense algorithms, the question of whether to borrow or not always comes down to who's in charge: you or the money?

With us, it's never been a close call.

Life on Their Own Terms

Laura and Pete, like many entrepreneurs, have always been their own people. Joyce Connors, who did Laura and Pete's books in the early days, and who now owns the bakery in Bozeman, Montana, remembers her first impression of them.

"Back then there were hippies who were really into drugs and other ones who were into politics. But there was another group, the ones who were back-to-the-land types. That was definitely Laura and Pete. In that way, they were a lot like Mike and me. They didn't have a

TV—still don't as far as I know—and they didn't get a newspaper. All they wanted to do was hike in the mountains. I don't know if they had this simplicity thing going, or if they were just really cheap, but they never spent money on anything except outdoor gear. They had really good outdoor gear. They loved to take wilderness trips and go way back. They'd go up to the Northwest Territories and the Yukon all the time, fly in and canoe the Yellowknife or the Big Salmon for a couple of weeks. I always thought that was cool."

You see these values—a love of simplicity, self-reliance, a certain sense of adventure—pop up like perennial flowers in dozens of places in the company. Whether it is the simple, functional look of the franchise offices, the absence of fancy perks for employees, the way lots of people in the office are both granola-eaters *and* big-game hunters, or the simple, open look of our marketing materials, the company clearly manifests the founders' love of independence and simplicity.

In a letter to the small but growing circle of franchisees, Pete describes their early days in Dillon this way.

When we moved to Dillon exactly two years ago, we figured we'd just pick up a little place in the country and move in— had to be lots of places like that in a town like Dillon, right? Wrong. We moved four times from rental to rental, waiting for something to come up. Finally, when we got sick of that we bought raw land eight miles from town, picked up a 1926 farmhouse on rails, hauled it away, and plunked it out in our alfalfa field.

It's an old house, and it needs work, but it is just a great feeling to sit there and look out the window at the mountains and know that nobody can kick us out, that we can drive a nail into the wall anywhere we want. We bought our first dishwasher, which is such a treat that we argue over who gets to do the dishes. Finally, we have kids and horses and chickens and junk all collected in one place, and it sure feels fine.

We took a hike with some friends last Sunday, and saw the

first wildflowers of the season in the mountains—some little purple jobs, I forget what you call them. It was freezing and I had to give it to them for being out at all. The snow is melting fast here, though, and we've got our traditional bear hunting trip planned for the first weekend in May—this trip always deteriorates into Dad and Mom drinking beer and eating T-bones and sleeping a lot and spoiling the kids and the horses, so nobody need worry on behalf of the bears.

Happiness, Revisited

Laura and Pete have always been content, happy people, which is an accomplishment if you think about it. How many of your friends can you say are really content or happy? Our evening together in Papa T's is winding down and I have one more question to ask.

"What makes for a good day?" I begin. "You seem like you try to live life fully."

"No," says Pete, surprising me with the passion in his voice, "I actually hate that whole *carpe diem*, live-each-day-to-the-fullest thing. I believe in the magic of the everyday. Take the most ordinary moment you can imagine—just us sitting here, for example. It's a miracle. It actually is the most miraculous moment you can possibly imagine. Then take another moment in your life, like when Valerie was born, when all the forces of life just came together in a split second. Or maybe it's a bad moment like an auto accident, something really intense, and see it as a completely ordinary moment. That's what life is. Completely ordinary and yet magical and amazing and life-changing at the same time. The ordinary is a total miracle and the most miraculous thing is totally ordinary. That's where I end. I get to be totally in love with and awed by a single day, even, and maybe in particular, a perfectly ordinary day. I get to avoid the pressure of the *carpe diem* thing and instead simply get to have a quiet day with Laura where we go for a walk or something."

Laura laughs and says, "Pete, I can't believe you are saying that. You are one of the most *carpe diem* people I know in that you refuse to do something you don't want to do."

"Yeah, I do what I feel like doing," he starts, taking a sip from his beer and warming to the subject. "The fact is that Laura and I spend a whole lot more time than most people just asking ourselves, 'What do we really want to do?' Then we go do it. A lot of people think that looking at the world that way is selfish, but they're wrong. It turns out that the question 'What do I want to do?' has a strange nested quality about it, and maybe that is what confuses so many people. What you feel like doing in this minute must coexist with the things you feel like doing in the coming hour, day, week, month, year, five years, and twenty years. This is why it often feels as though you aren't doing what you want, when really you are. You have to be pretty adept to see each day as truly yours with all those nested wants."

We're all quiet for a moment as we ponder this idea that happiness-in-a-day is some sort of Russian doll-within-a-doll. Laura finally breaks our reverie, softly adding a last thought: "To me there are all kinds of perfect days. Like yesterday was a perfect day because we went skiing all day and it was really fun. Today was a perfect day. I was just happy to be here. Any day can be perfect. You decide to be happy with it. You make a *commitment* to be happy with it, and when you do, those are the good days."

We call it a night, and they bundle up and make their way out into the new snow. It has been a good night.

. . .

I love telling the story of Laura and Pete. It's a good story, full of quirkiness and success, close calls and romance, but I suspect I like it also because it is a story I wish I could tell about myself. My story, of course, is different and somewhat less compelling. I grew up in suburban Northern Virginia—a land that no one is really from. I went to high school there and then college in Ohio, an uninspired student, floating along most of the way, not at all sure what I wanted to do with my life. When I finally hit my professional stride—first working for a politician, then going overseas to the Baltics, and finally joining Great Harvest, I was doing good work, but never felt quite satisfied. It is funny how you can be doing well—making money, buying that first house, having kids, and all the while you grow slightly more crazy every day, the drops of dissatisfaction pooling around your feet like wasted sweat.

In good moments, I call myself a "seeker," someone walking through life asking lots of good questions. But in low moments, I secretly wonder if I am just a dilettante, destined to try lots of things, but never be much good at any one, mired, ultimately, in a kind of existential limbo. It isn't that I don't have good moments. I do—lots of them, really. It is just that I have this nagging fear that there is nothing coherent tying all the moments together. I feel like I need structure, or at least answers.

The biggest outward manifestation of all this is the way I frenetically bounce from one project to the next. One day, I want to transform the way Great Harvest does promotion, the next I am going to be the best parent ever—dedicated to teaching Valerie how to read and speak French. But none of it lasts. It is all sound and fury, but not much work on the really important and very little peace if any. And then there is the driving but unfocused ambition, that nagging feeling that I should be doing something important with my life, but little clarity on what that something is.

I have a sense that I would profit from a mentor, someone to show me the way, but no one is exactly jumping out of the woodwork to take on my case. I do know we are all surrounded by teachers, if we are willing to learn. There aren't a lot of people who know what the whole puzzle looks like, but I've begun to see there are lots of people who know where individual pieces of the puzzle fit. I tell myself to keep looking and asking questions. Maybe I will be surprised at how it all adds up.

5

FACING CRISIS

As the franchise continued to grow, Laura and Pete added more employees. The growing size of the company was fun. Now it wasn't just the two of them, alone in an office calling bakery owners on the phone, but a burgeoning community of colleagues.

Systems

Employees, however, brought their own challenges. Quickly, Laura and Pete realized that in order to grow and keep any control of their lives, they needed to create systems for running the business. Systems give you freedom—you can leave your business in the hands of others and know it will be well run—and they also give you security, for a business with strong systems is better able to withstand the inevitable challenges that come along.

It was about this time that Laura and Pete's summer vacations became formalized. They had always taken off on long vacations—a month or so—but now these vacations became the rule. They were gone from June through August every year. They hiked the old Yellowstone to Glacier trail again, but this time they did the 500 miles with their teenage girls. They learned Spanish and went to hike in Bolivia and Ecuador. It was becoming more and more possible to do their own thing for longer periods of time.

Owners of other businesses ask them how they can possibly manage to be gone from the business for so long. Their answer has always been the same: "systems." As Michael Gerber, author of *The E-Myth*, puts it, the goal is to "work on the business, not just in the business." Focusing on systems, however, is difficult, harder than blaming your people for making mistakes. But, reports Director of Franchise Services and long-time Great Harvest employee, Debbie Harrison Huber, Laura and Pete work to avoid this trap. "Nothing is ever personal with them. If you make a mistake, it is because a *system* is missing, not because you messed up."

Systems came easily to Laura and Pete. On some basic level, franchising is all about systems. You reduce the operations of a small business to its essential elements with an eye toward reproducing your first success. As Great Harvest got larger, Laura and Pete focused their talent for producing bakery operating procedures on the franchise business itself, creating hiring checklists, budget checklists, bakery visit checklist, and new candidate selection checklists. Debbie explains, "In the words of Jim Collins and Jerry Porras, authors of *Built to Last*, Laura and Pete tried hard to be clockmakers and not just timekeepers. Neither of them are big charismatic leaders, but that tends to be a good thing for the company. The company has learned not to depend on them as leaders. Instead, we are forever building systems—for finding good people, for running stores, and for profit-making. The result is impressive for a company our size. We could be doing all this by the seat of our pants, but instead we are learning, refining and, in the process, building a company that will outlast any of us." Systems, I am learning, are central to building a strong and sustainable company.

For Pete, creating systems became a game. If he and Laura could invent a system that would allow the two of them to do whatever they wanted whenever they wanted, they won. One morning I stopped by his small office on the second floor of our building in Dillon and he told me of the time he rode up a chair lift with Yvon Chouinard, the founder of Patagonia. "He's one of my heroes. He said the best thing that ever happened to him in business was surfing, because you never know when the surf's up. You can't predict it. You can't say, 'February fourteenth I am going surfing on some big waves. In order to surf big waves, you have to arrange your whole business around being able to take off anytime you want. You have to be able to take off with one day or even an hour's notice. And that makes you smart about creating systems that don't require your constant presence.' "

To this day, Great Harvest has a strong culture of checklists. "Systems make you free," we preach to new franchisees. "Without them, you are simply baking bread and training new counter people. With them, you are able to think about growing the business and taking time off with your family."

Getting Help

But even with all the systems, the Wakemans started to think in terms of bringing on someone who could run the operation in their absence. The two of them were still personally opening most of the stores—Laura would fly out for opening days and Pete would stick around as the "long trainer." In 1988, they decided to get some help. "We needed someone who could do what we were doing, not just be support help," remembers Laura. Their advertisement in the *Wall Street Journal* brought a flood of responses. "All we did was advertise a good little job, decent pay, and limited hours in a pretty part of the country," Laura says "and the response was unbelievable." Eventually, after much soul-searching, they hired Ray Potter, an MBA originally from Michigan.

"Ray was a personality," recalls Joyce Conners, who by this time was the company's top financial person. "He was one of a kind. In a lot of ways he was really good for the franchise. He introduced the idea of promoting bakeries to their communities and helped systematize openings. This was just about the time when bread started becoming trendy. We were getting some big openings. I think a lot of what he did was important, but he had a way of upsetting people. He had a really big ego. It was about this time that Pete started working at home. I always got the feeling that he just couldn't stand Ray. Ray and Laura would get along really well, but they'd also fight—big fights. It got to be hard on everyone here in Dillon."

The rift that grew between Ray and the Wakemans shook the company. Looking back at this time, I realize businesses are like relationships—they aren't really worth much until they have endured their first good crisis. We all know people who are still courting—everything's great. Both people adore each other. The other person can do no wrong. But is it real? Or is it just the first blush of a wonderful enthusiasm? Until a business has been tested, no one can be really sure if it will last.

Finally, it was too much. Ray quit or was fired, depending on whom you talk with, in early 1992. Soon thereafter, two other experienced trainers left as well. It was Great Harvest's first taste of crisis. All three wanted to start their own bakeries, but Laura and Pete said no, feeling their process for opening bakeries was proprietary. It was an ugly time with most of the company's energy going into one painful separation after another. Ultimately, the franchise sued one of the former employees for misappropriation of trade secrets. Laura looks at it today with some perspective. "We certainly got ourselves an education throughout all that." But in hindsight, some sort of crisis was inevitable. Would-be entrepreneurs are wise to expect it.

Focus on Health

Writing at the time, Pete sounds tired:

> Building a company is the hardest thing Laura and I have ever done. This company, as it grows, is incredibly difficult to run. We're proud of it, and we're very happy—rightfully so—but we're tired.
>
> Our people are tired, too. We just lost one of our best people, and are in the process of losing two more. When you have so many people involved in a thing, and you want to make it good for everyone, no exceptions, it gets very confusing. Mostly, we fall back on an instinct for health. We're healthy ourselves, and we think we have a good handle on health in business, too. When someone wants something that may be good for them, but will make all of Great Harvest unhealthy, we look for alternatives. It's been terribly hard on everyone here. For those who remain with us, there's constant, constant, constant change. Change is great, but people need just a little break sometimes. Weekly change would be a breath of fresh air, right now.
>
> I badly need a vacation. Laura does, too. We're going to Mexico, to a little cattle and mining town smaller than Dillon, where there's no motel and only a few stores. We'll have to stay in a Mexican house with a Mexican family and eat nothing but Mexican food and not even talk English, let alone Great Harvest. We're psyched as can be, just to go do something totally different.

Give Your People the Chance
to Build the Systems

I look back on this time—everyone left a year before I arrived—and wonder what could have gone so wrong. Was this not the fairy-tale company I had so eagerly described to Mary when we were camped out in Missoula looking for work? My best guess as to why the three left comes from the frustrations I feel some days. One of the bad things about working for a company that starts other little companies is that it is hard to keep from wanting one of your own. Running your own thing looks like fun. And systems—as good as they are—can make people feel like they are not contributing. The same checklists that free an owner to leave a store, knowing things will run the same as if they were there, can slowly deaden the souls of those charged with working down the page of tasks to be completed. I remember commiserating with another Great Harvester a couple of years back. He said to me, "Systems, systems, systems. That's all we ever hear. What's the goal here, to nail down the operations of this company so that a trained monkey could run it while Laura and Pete are out of town?" The answer is, "No," of course. The reason for systems is to free everyone so they can apply their best thinking to the problems that haven't yet been solved. But I knew where this guy was coming from, and I'll bet Ray and those two trainers did too. The lesson for entrepreneurs is to be careful to give employees an active hand in creating the systems they are being asked to work lest they think their talents are being underused.

Cash

In addition to having strong systems, one of the main reasons Great Harvest was able to survive the loss of three key people and indeed to thrive was the fact that Laura and Pete had no debt and had built big cash reserves. With crisis at the door, suddenly their pay-as-you-go approach began to look like prescient business strategy. It proved to be sound insurance against inevitable challenges.

What might well have brought down a more fragile business did not derail the company. Indeed, 1992 and 1993 brought more new hires, many of them young people, and a fresh excitement to the Dillon office. It also proved the soundness of the basic Great Harvest structure and the uniqueness of the product. We'll take a look at that structure first and see that this form of community produces advantages needed by all sorts of organizations in our society today. Next, we'll discover how Great Harvest attracts great people to our enterprise at a time when lots of employment opportunities beckon.

.   .   .

I wasn't working for Great Harvest during the "great upheaval," but it must have been hard on everyone. Here was this little company just bopping along, and suddenly it is split by forces seemingly beyond its control. I know if it had been my company, I would have been honestly scared—that everything would fly apart and that I would lose what represented fifteen years of work. But people who were there tell me that throughout those months, Laura and Pete continued to demonstrate one of their most admirable qualities: fearlessness.

Being completely without fear is more unusual than you might think. Everyone is always talking about being scared of something— that they are going to lose their job, their business will go down, their kid will get kidnapped at the mall, or that no one will like them anymore. Human beings seem supernaturally creative when it comes to inventing fears. I know I am. I worry that I won't be able to pay for the kids' college, that I will grow mediocre in my job, that I will grow lazy in my relationship with Mary. But not Laura and Pete. Sometimes I'll catch them talking about this whole freedom franchise thing is a "big experiment," wondering out loud "how it will all turn out." They're famous for saying, "It's only a job. It's a good job, but we could always find another if we had to." It's unsettling sometimes. I, for one, am not used to my bosses talking casually, even indifferently, about the worst case. I've actually grown dependent on someone who is older and more powerful telling me it will all work out okay.

Fear is bad for business. When people are fearful, they retreat into their small selves. Fear is the emotion that sits behind greed, anger, and hatred, none of which adds value to the world. In the absence of fear, however, people are their most creative. They give of themselves more fully and are able to work with others without being hobbled by worries about how they are perceived.

I was talking to Susan Downer, our wheat manager, the other day. She was telling me that 1 John 4:18 was one of her favorite lines in the Bible. We were driving up to check on the wheat crop north of Great Falls, and she had a Bible in the truck, so we looked it up. The verse says, "There is no fear in love. Perfect love drives out fear. . . ." That seems about right: love and fear, locked in a zero sum contest. The more we fret about the future, the less we are able to love the present, and the more we love who we are and what we do, the less room in our hearts for fear.

It's hard to see what this has to do with business, but it has everything to do with it. Fear is ugly and turns people off, while love—love of other people, love of what we are able to create, love of what we do—is enormously, even magically, attractive. Business is nothing if it is not all about being attractive. That's doubly true for a retail or service business, which is all about people. Being nearly perfectly fearless is one of the most important attributes Laura and Pete model for the rest of us. In their freedom from fear, they make way for love.

6

BUILDING FREEDOM
INTO THE BUSINESS

L ast week I flew in from visiting bakeries on the East Coast. In long-term parking at the Idaho Falls airport, my old Ford pickup was covered in snow. I scraped off the windshield with a credit card and began my drive north across Monida Pass toward Dillon. Around Dubois, I turned Sheryl Crow down on the CD player and wondered again if entrepreneurs were the only ones who can live a life of real freedom. I sure hope not. It'd be nice if the rest of us—the teachers, the corporate employees, and the organization women and men—could have a shot at it.

I decide for my own mental health that we can.

Freedom and Happiness Are
Available to All

Freedom is a state of mind. Even if our high school guidance counselors told us we weren't likely to amount to much, or if we're trapped in a workaholic company any of us can choose to feel free whenever we want. I am sure of it. The joy and freedom I saw in Terri Winn and Brian Turner's eyes on opening day is like being in shape. It's a choice. Laura and Pete are free because they chose to live in Montana and chose to start a little business that would support their lives. The day we decide to design our lives from the ground up is the day we become free. Of course, lots of people don't see it that way. Frequently, I don't. Many days I see my life as a series of stage directions given to me by the unseen hand of circumstance, but it's true. We're as free as a kid on a playground at recess.

I wheeled my way over the pass and was glad I'd piled big rocks in the back of the pickup to weight it down and better pin it to the road. The snow was starting to pick up.

This connection between freedom and happiness gets right to the heart of why Great Harvest is organized the way it is. Great Harvest feels freedom is the ground on which happiness stands, and so it is organized in a way that provides store owners maximum freedom. While freedom is a state of mind—an understanding that we can choose who we are and what we do—it is also more. It is a condition. It is real—something you can measure. People who lived in Latvia under Soviet rule can measure, and appreciate, how much freedom they have now versus how much they had before the Iron Curtain came down.

If Great Harvest cares about the happiness of our owners, we have two jobs: to encourage store owners to see their lives as a choice, *and* to build a truly free system that encourages them to make choices both culturally and structurally. Much of our passion in Dillon is directed toward this latter work.

Franchising—A Way to Be
Your Own Boss

There are currently 1,500 franchises operating in the United States today and many more overseas. Most of them are "business format" franchises, meaning they offer guidance for how to run a certain type of enterprise. Great Harvest Bread Co. is a business format franchise.

If I took a poll of all the people in our system, most would say our core purpose is selling great bread in a unique and authentic retail store. Real bread from real people.

But in Dillon, we have another aim as well, to teach people how to create that retail magic. As much as we love the bread biz, we love the franchising side of our work just as much.

And who wouldn't love it? We make dreams come true. Talk to any franchiser, and they'll tell you the same thing. At a recent International Franchise Association convention, I was huddled with a group of franchising bigwigs and the talk turned to what we do. A satisfied glow settled over our little group.

"Everyone wants to be their own boss. My job is to help make it happen," said one VP of operations.

"We think of our franchise as a center of entrepreneurial development where we help people realize their dreams," added a CEO and franchise founder.

It is a happy little fraternity, really. These supposedly hard-edged business people grow warm and excited when talking about how much fun it is to help people go into business for themselves. For many would-be entrepreneurs, teaming up with a franchiser already active in the work that interests them is a smart move. They'll be in business *for* themselves, but not *by* themselves.

Some of our best days at the Great Harvest office in Dillon occur during our week-long training sessions for new owners. Each one is full of hope and energy, like proud parents picking out curtains for the nursery. Says Dawn Eisenzimer, who works in Dillon on legal affairs, "They bring to the table their town, their local knowledge, their drive, and passion, and we bring twenty-five years of experience about how to run this business. Together, we are capable of really good things." Emotions run high during these periodic Dillon Training Weeks as together we envision what we are going to do as a team.

A Freedom Franchise—Liberty as the Highest Value

As much as we are like other franchisers, we're different in an important way. Most franchises begin when someone—call them the founder—figures out a way to sell a bunch of doughnuts or smoothies in a compelling way, writes the method down and then invites others to copy what she or he has done.

The great thing about opening a store with this sort of franchise is that you aren't taking on much risk. The business is proven. You'll almost surely make money. The bad thing, if you're a truly entrepreneurial type, is that you won't have much fun. All the good stuff about opening your own business—figuring out everything from what you want to offer to what color the walls will be—aren't your decisions to make. They've already been made by Mr. or Mrs. Founder. You'll discover in your franchise's headlong pursuit of a consistent brand image, the business is pretty unwilling to have you fool with the founder's blueprint.

An alternative to being part of a franchise—if you want to own your own small business—is to open a Mom and Pop store. The good part is you decide on your product line, your hours of operation, and whether your counter people will wear tie-dyed shirts or snappy little baseball caps with your logo on them. The bad thing is that most small businesses fail because their owners are unable to overcome the rush of challenges that face any new businessperson. Taxes, promotion, hiring, and back office systems each wait to trip you up. It's not that a smart person like you can't figure these things out—you can—it is just a question of whether you have the energy to do so. The challenges just keep coming, one after another, wearing you down after a while. If you are trying to create a life that has space for your spouse, your kids, and yourself, it is nearly impossible. You're on your own, flying solo with no one else to help out in the cockpit when you're ready for a nap. That tires most businesspeople out after a while, and it's why so many startups fail.

Great Harvest occupies the middle ground between joining a franchise and going out on your own. Our goal is to create a *community* of Mom and Pop operators—each free to create their stores as they please, and each contributing to a pool of expertise that is available to all—something we call a freedom franchise.

In an old promotional brochure, Pete put it this way: "The culture of Great Harvest comes out of a dynamic tension between two antagonistic ideals. On the one hand, we love *quality*. We are stubbornly opinionated about the best way to run a bread company. Taken by itself, this idea would lead to an autocratic operation committed to strict quality standards, uniformly enforced on all franchisees. We have a second ideal, equally strong, however. We believe that no person, society, or institution can be great without *liberty*. In our hierarchy of values, freedom is at the top; ahead of money, ahead of security, ahead of comfort, ahead of any of the things that people strive for."

Owners of Great Harvest Bread Co.s have perfect freedom to create their stores as they please, even the freedom to make bad decisions or ultimately to fail. But they aren't on their own. They run their bakeries within a community of like-minded owners each struggling with the same challenges and each bringing different talents to the job. They stand on the shoulders of 250 owners and twenty-plus years of experience.

You know the old business saying? When in doubt, check the contract. Here's what ours says:

ANYTHING
not expressly prohibited by
the language of this agreement
IS ALLOWED

That is pretty much heresy in the world of traditional franchising where command and control are the order of the day. It turns the normal world of franchising—"do it our way unless you can convince us otherwise"—on its head.

I've had skeptical people ask me if Great Harvest owners are really free. "Surely, you must have some standards." And it is true we have a handful. Every Great Harvest owner must display the Great Harvest sign and marks in their store. Also, they have to fresh-mill their flour on premises and buy premium wheat from approved suppliers, but that is about it. Our contract says nothing about recipes or store design or product selection. That is left completely to the owner.

Why This Is Important—A New Way to Organize

I love this idea of a freedom franchise—a loose confederation of people independently tackling similar problems but connected strongly together in a network. I love it because this form of association leaves room for personality and freedom while effectively creating innovation and change through collaboration. You can see its potential—schools run as teacher-nets, labs run as engineer-nets, and synods run as minister-nets. I can't help but feel like Great Harvest is part of a small, but growing, class of organizations that is thinking hard about how to balance the need to be freely creative and the desire to be part of a community and doing so successfully by creating small groups of richly cross-linked, dispersed free networks.

Tom and Sally—
Yearning to Be Free

Tom Amundson and Sally Weissman have owned their bakery in Minneapolis for eighteen years. They are some of the system's fore-bearers, having begat the begats who begat the current generation of store owners. In the system they are known simply as Tom and Sally. Their example is what makes Great Harvest much of what it is.

Tom is an athlete. Not the big, well-muscled type, but the slim and flexible sort you find warming up at weekend cross-country run-ning matches. His new love is speed skating, a sport he enjoys with his young teenaged son, Robbie.

I love Tom for the twinkle in his eye. When we say in our mission statement, "Be Loose and Have Fun," most of us think of Tom. Not that he doesn't have his serious side. He's all purpose when talking about how to regrind the furrows on a big thirty-inch stone mill, but that whimsical side is never far away. I've found Tom easy to be with since the day we first met.

Sally is equally focused, but in a different, quieter way. Slight, with medium-length brown hair, she possesses the kind of mind that's fun to watch. She used to be a cash commodities trader, and you can see why. She's as quick as sunlight shimmering off a windy lake, with an intelligence that just brightens your day.

Together, Tom and Sally are highly effective. The Upton Avenue bakery in Minneapolis has consistently been one of the system's high-est grossing bakeries. When we talk about creating retail magic in stores or baking bread that just blows people away, the Minneapolis example is never far from our minds.

I recently spent an hour talking with Tom and Sally in their home. They own a simple blue-and-white frame house a couple of blocks from the bakery. Tom had just returned from a run and was in the shower when I arrived. Sally got me a glass of cold water. We sat down in their living room and I asked them to tell me their Great Harvest "story."

Sally started, "Well, you know I grew up in Great Falls. I'd go home to my folks' house from Minneapolis where I was working and get bread over at Holliday Village. Laura and Pete owned the bakery then, and they would have long tables set out in the mall and would slice big free slices for all comers. That was my first taste. It was 1976. We just loved the bread. We got my brother Jeff to overnight the bread to us in Minneapolis. That and the cinnamon rolls. It got to the point where it was the only thing we ate. We loved to run and would go for fifteen mile runs on the weekend and eat a whole cinnamon roll when we got done."

Tom smiles, remembering, and then adds, "I always knew I wanted to be in business for myself. When Sally and I got married, it suddenly seemed possible, like together we could do it. We started looking at different businesses, but just kept coming back to Great Harvest. . . ."

Says Sally, "We really wanted a product we could believe in, something that would allow us to lead our healthy lifestyle."

"One day we were talking to Jeff about this," Tom continues, "and he said, 'Great Harvest's a franchise. You should call them.' So we did. From the start we looked at the business as a way to support the way we wanted to live our lives. Money was never the main thing. We figured if we made money, fine, but our real goals were *to be our own boss and to have the freedom to do our thing*."

"We didn't want to work for someone else," remembers Sally. "We were tired of the politics. I was one of the first women to be hired by my company as a professional. After doing that for a while, I just wanted to be independent. To me, happiness is total freedom to do what you want. There are always things you have to do, of course, but I wanted freedom to make choices."

Skating Close to the Edge

Being part of a freedom franchise is a dangerous thing. There are no guarantees. As Pete writes in our promotional brochure, "We are not selling 'success' or 'security.' A near-guarantee of success, such as other well-run franchises offer, is a very different thing from a guarantee of freedom. The two don't mix. Even a franchise that allows a lot of innovation from its strongest franchisees, while paternalistically protecting its weaker members from making mistakes, is fooling nobody on the price paid in freedom to buy security. Freedom isn't 'the right to do anything you want, as long as you show the home office you're being sensible.' That's a phony approximation of working for yourself—safer, maybe, but not freedom. Freedom has always been, and always will be, the freedom to do what you think is right without justifying it first to others."

We've had our share of store failures over the years. Some of the earliest store closures were because of divorce. Running a small business is never gentle on relationships. Today store closures tend to be for two reasons: the business doesn't turn out to be a good fit with its owners, no matter how much homework we've all done, or people decide they don't need the franchise to succeed. This latter drive is the dark side of the freedom franchise. Recruit strong, independent people in love with making their own choices, and some will eventually want to be completely free of any group. This is definitely a weakness in our system. The ties that bind the group together find their roots less in contract law than they do in common purpose, which while strategically stronger is structurally weaker.

So why do this? Why organize a freedom franchise? Does this form of community have advantages not found elsewhere? The answer is yes.

.   .   .

I'm feeling lucky today. I have a lot of heroes in my life. How many people are blessed with as many role models as I have, people like Laura and Pete, or Tom and Sally? Who can look at Barry Sparks, owner of two stores in Denver, and not be inspired by the lightness with which he holds the world? Or by the compassion that Mike and Julie Scheel bring to their businesses in Salem, Oregon? Increasingly, I know I can't "do" life on my own. I need community. It supports me and makes me a little less lonely. And it gives me a chance to ask the important questions of my life.

But that said, I have to admit, I'm feeling increasingly restless at Great Harvest. I have start-up lust. All I can think about these days is opening my own store or going into business for myself. Working for someone else isn't always fun. Laura and Pete are good people, but as Pete said, "Even in those days, there was flat no way I was going to work for somebody else." The urge to do your own thing is powerful and hard to resist.

It is a frustration that comes on like the dark clouds that blow into Dillon from the north. It will be blue and sunny one moment. I'll be doing the work of the franchise, helping someone open a bakery or thinking hard about where we should be committing research and development dollars. Then the wind will pick up and suddenly it's overcast and gloomy. Who's to say where it starts? Where do clouds come from anyway? Somewhere off the edge of consciousness, down where the air is cold and the way not known.

Part of me thinks it is Ego. Me. Me. Me. I want to do it my way. I want to be the boss. I don't want anyone telling me what to do. But part of me says it is simply the desire to create. They say God is unknowable. The ancient Jews called God Yahweh, or that which cannot be named. But I think in the act of creation—in our own little reenactments of the Genesis story—we can know God. Yesterday, Valerie brought home a simple little drawing of two horses made with brown crayons. These were her first horses, and they brought tears to my eyes as I saw her pride and wonder at this thing she had made.

So maybe the desire to do my own thing isn't all Ego. Maybe a part of it is the more noble instinct to share with the world that which is uniquely mine. People need the chance to create things in their own image. Indeed, I need that opportunity. I need that chance to know God, even if it is only every once in a while.

It is not that I don't still love this place, it is just that I am starting to wonder if the grass might not be greener on the other side of the fence. I put my résumé on the Internet the other day just to see what would come back. I thought of it as a kind of harmless, anonymous trolling. Of course I got caught. It wasn't a week before Ed Kerpius, a smart and funny owner in Philadelphia, called me up and said, "So, I see you are looking. . . ." I told him I wasn't looking, but I am not so sure. I'd better start being more careful.

7

THE TIPI PRINCIPLE: HOW FREEDOM CREATES COMPETITIVE ADVANTAGE

I didn't go to business school and I didn't take any classes on business during college. If I know anything about business, I learned it somewhere else. Like the year my friend Steve Morris and I lived in a tipi.

It was our senior year at Oberlin College. We wanted to live in a tipi because it represented a simpler way of life, a regime of splitting wood, cooking over an open fire, and entertaining ourselves with the sounds of wind, rain, and rustling trees. A funny thing happened, though, as our year of living simply wore on. Our tipi turned out to be strongly magnetic, causing all sorts of people—old men out birding, little kids playing army, couples taking romantic strolls—to stop by and visit. It was as if we lived in a giant conversation piece. Bit by bit, and then quickly, our big white tipi introduced us to most of our neighbors.

That tipi taught me a lesson: opportunities are often attractive for one reason, but end up being good for quite another. New products or processes with obvious advantages turn out to be boons for entirely different reasons. Call it the Tipi Principle: if you stay loose and roll with an idea, opportunity often edges out planned-for results.

This has certainly been true with Great Harvest and franchising. We turned to franchising first as a way to give people a chance to be their own bosses and to grow the whole without going into debt. Today, however, we see franchising less as a method to raise cash for growth and more as a way to create authentic stores and gather smart people together and turn their energy and vision into competitive advantage.

When other franchisers come to visit us in Dillon, they are quick to wonder why we have abandoned what they see as the only motive to franchise—brand consistency. Here's our answer.

Two Reasons to Be a Freedom Franchise

First, being a freedom franchise allows us to learn quickly and adapt rapidly to a changing marketplace.

I have two friends—one works in a big company and the other owns his own bike shop. Their problems couldn't be more different. The woman who works for the big company says she loves it—she's forever bumping into really smart people, which causes her to bubble over with ideas about how to improve the business. Problem is, she says, she has little authority to make anything happen. "I'm a marketing person," she laments, "and even more accurately, my job is to worry about buying advertising. If I have an idea for how to articulate our points of difference in the marketplace more effectively, or an idea about how to streamline production, I am powerless to implement them. That's not my job. It is someone else's."

My bike shop friend has the opposite problem. "I'm here by myself for much of the day," he reports. "I have all the power in the world to do whatever I want, but it is hard to get inspired. It is difficult to find time to read business books or travel to small business conventions, much less talk to other small bike shop owners, who on some level I view as competition."

One of the things that makes Great Harvest hum is that owners of bread stores have the best of both worlds—they are in close association with others who are doing exactly what they are doing, and this proximity sparks in them all sorts of interesting ideas. But they also are completely autonomous, free to implement in their stores the ideas that excite them. Being organized as a freedom franchise allows all of us in Great Harvest to combine *quick learning with the power of rapid adaptation.*

Leveraging Community

Last year when speaking to a business class in Vermont, I was asked to describe Great Harvest in a single phrase. It took me off guard. It is hard to sum up years of work in a single string of words. I came up with this: "We are a for-profit guild of whole-wheat bread bakers." I like that word "guild." It brings to mind a free association of tradespeople committed to the betterment of their craft.

Creating and encouraging this learning community is at the center of our strategy. There are two types of business—ones that concentrate on bringing new products to market and those that come in later and provide those goods or services for a lower price. We want to be among the market makers, not among the low-cost duplicators. We've always admired Sony because they produce products that customers don't even know they want yet. Business legend has it that when Sony tested its Walkman, the market research folks concluded it would never sell. But Sony produced it anyway, confident of its vision. We want to be that type of company, one that is creating the future, not shaving pennies off the past.

In franchising this re-invention doesn't come easily. The industry is littered with concepts that burn brightly for ten years, then flame out as the newest thing edges them from the marketplace. The greatness of that original business idea can be a trap that leads you toward thinking the first way something was done is the best way. It is critical in this business to figure out a way continually to invent the future. To do this, large top-down franchises establish research and development departments to create new products and test different ways to sell them.

Research and Development, Great Harvest Style

At Great Harvest, we're going in a different direction with our freedom franchise idea. We connect our independent Moms and Pops together into what we call the "learning community." This results in all sorts of invention and self-regeneration as the system finds out what works in the marketplace and what doesn't.

The result of all this de-centralization is dozens of experiments all happening at once with no one really in charge and a system that is by its very nature continually renewing itself. By joining owners together, we profit from 250 minds all working independently on how to make this business better and don't find ourselves relying on two or three headquarters types who have sole charge of research and development.

It is an enormously stable form of organization. Explains Pete,

All of this has a dramatic and dangerous sound. On the contrary, it is the only course of safety, and will make us wildly successful and unstoppable as a group. Hit us with something bad and we are multi-redundant, quickly self-healing any breach in the cross-linked net. Throw us a problem and 100 separate eight- to twelve-member groups work in parallel to solve it, with head-spinning speed. Send the whole system in the wrong direction, and renegade groups quietly assemble, perfect, and prove themselves, until the system turns. Change the whole world all at once, we reconfigure, transmute, then emerge again reborn brand new.

The Strategy of Cross Fertilization

The freedom guaranteed in our franchising contract means there are no rules for owners to follow when operating their businesses. The franchise company conducts no inspections to make sure a franchisee is complying with "the blueprint." Instead, owners take the original idea of what a Great Harvest bakery should be, tweak it, apply it in new ways, and in general add a little of themselves to it. And they talk and share ideas. In a variant on Darwin's law, only the exciting and most profitable ideas survive. It's like a marketplace of bakery tips where the only currency is successful use.

- A baker in Evanston, Illinois, invents a new bread called Apple Scrapple. It's so good it's addictive. The Evanston owner casually mentions the success he has been having with Apple Scrapple to an owner-friend in Virginia who then tries it himself. At the next meeting of his owner peer group, this second owner shares his success with the bread. They try the recipe and like it. Inside a month, more than half the system is offering it to the public.

- Two new owners from Nebraska talk about a new promotion they've heard of where the bakery donates the proceeds from a day's production to a local school group. In quick order, the idea spreads to Colorado, then Salt Lake and on to Kansas City. Proceeds help a local playground, a children's camp, and a program for the blind. The idea is written up in the newsletter. Dozens use the idea in the coming months with good success.

Our job as franchiser is to create lots of opportunities for owners to exchange ideas. We organize conventions, host regional meetings, hold owner-led trainings, sponsor group buying and marketing co-operatives, pay for owners to visit each other's stores, write newsletters, and connect owners together online using chat sessions and discussion groups.

Like many franchise companies and chains, we have a team of field representatives that fan out across the country and visit bakeries. What our field representatives do on those visits, however, is different. Their aim is not to assess how well an owner is complying with the corporate manual, but to act as bees, buzzing from bloom to bloom, cross pollinating as they go, making sure knowledge passes from bakery to bakery.

The "cross travel" program is one of my favorites. We have a standing offer to pay for half of any travel in our system. If an owner or employee visits another bakery, we'll pay for half of their travel and expenses. No questions asked. No reports. No permission. We do this because we know when owners and employees visit different bakeries, everyone learns something. Which makes the system smarter.

All these connections ignite sparks around the network which keep us fresh.

I saw Pete in his office the other day and we got to talking about the learning community. He told me, "Our job is to invent, as a group, a radical totally new system of organization that is neither franchise, company, or community, but similar to each—*an adaptive net,* centered around *fast learning* as the core value. Learning as what we do, learning as our source of fun, learning as the source of all our innovation, and learning as the key to our success."

Computers help us with this cross-fertilization. For years now we've had e-mail. Owners go online to chat with fellow bakers. Topics range from good deals on equipment to the best ways to find employees in a tight market. Two years ago, we created a members-only Web site called the extranet (an intranet but with remote access). It features chat rooms, discussion threads, system announcements, articles, and a full archive of old material. All these help us contribute easily, learn quickly, adapt to changing conditions, and keep ourselves fresh—Pete's "adaptive net."

The Adaptive Net Tackles Happiness

I once asked Pete what he envisioned for Great Harvest and he told me he saw two purposes for Great Harvest—to create a community in which we could all grow smarter at this thing called business, and to create a community of happy seekers, people who were genuinely interested in learning about how to live a good life.

It's happened. A public discourse occurs in Great Harvest on the best promotions and the best suppliers of walnuts, but at the same time conversations take place on how best to balance our lives with our businesses, how to pass on the value of hard work to our kids, and how to find happiness in a confusing world. It's fun and as important a part of who we are as all the "what's-the-best-cheddar-garlic-recipe" chatter. Life-balance and parenting workshops are consistently more popular than business topics at our annual convention, which tells you what people care about most.

A second advantage we have come to find in our form of franchising is: All of our stores are different, which means they are more authentic and attractive.

The biggest advantage to having a group of stores where everyone is free to do their own thing is that each store is unique, created in the image of its owners and of its community. This produces a kind of authenticity that is lacking in just about every other chain retail shop I visit.

For a long time, homogeneity seemed like the very face of modernity—crisp white paper caps that looked like partially opened envelopes perched jauntily on the heads of scrubbed teenagers serving up exactly the same burger you ate a week ago a thousand miles away. Progress.

But after fifty years of this, people are starting to pine after something different in the stores they patronize: Personality.

Oases of 100% Real

If you ever find yourself in San Francisco, check out North Beach's Café Italia. It's a real Italian café, airlifted straight from downtown Rome. Not a replica, but the real thing. There is a soccer game on the TV in the corner, not because some restaurant "concept" designer thought it would be a nice touch, but because Café Italia's owner—a well-fed forty-five-year-old—wouldn't dream of missing a match. Then there is the wait staff. All are recent immigrants and barely able to speak English. Between the difficulty deciphering what they are saying and a menu that is only in Italian, you think you're in Florence wishing you had studied your Berlitz books a bit more diligently before you made the trip. And the food! Thick slabs of hard-crusted breads slathered with the freshest tomatoes and basil imaginable and bathed in dark, indulgent olive oil: my idea of heaven. Everything in the store communicates Italy, from the racks of fresh newspapers from Rome, to the soccer, to the coffee flown in from Florence. There are no compromises.

I know all this about the Café Italia because Lisa Allen and I—Lisa was our marketing person at the time and is now the owner of the store in Medford, Oregon—were in San Francisco a couple of years back looking to discover the secret of "authenticity." We always knew "realness"—the fact that we are a string of Mom and Pop shops—was important to our success. When we stumbled upon Café Italia, we knew had found a truly *authentic* Italian café. As hard as spots like these are to uncover, authentic restaurants and shops are special and are never hard to distinguish from their weak and bloodless cousins, the chain store. Walk down any city street and your eye instantly knows Mom and Pop as opposed to chain. The first feels alive, vibrant, fresh and interesting while the second looks cookie-cutter, slick and soul-less.

When I shop, 95 percent of the retail stores I go into could change hands tomorrow and I wouldn't be able to tell. The owners have succeeded in erasing any trace of their presence from the store. It gives the stores an antiseptic, highly homogenized feel. And yet we all know that our favorite stores are the ones where the owner is front and center greeting people as they walk in the door like a favorite uncle welcoming you into his home at Christmas. As a culture, we're sick of being Wal-Martized. We yearn for genuine, authentic stores, ones where you feel the presence of a single person's creative vision.

I asked Pete what he thought about creating authenticity and unsurprisingly he wrote back with passion.

> Collectively we are unique—in our bread, in our bakeries, in our franchise—which gives us a shot at doing what nobody else has yet pulled off: the creation of myriad oases of 100% *real* all over the country.
>
> Our bread isn't white or sugary. Our bakeries aren't quiet or predictable. Our franchise isn't a franchise; it's an amalgamation of characters.
>
> The bigger a thing is, the more plastic it becomes, almost always. As we grow, protecting real authenticity at all levels of our business will call for more and more creativity, more things to try that have never been tried before. I'm an evangelist for the 100% Real. That's what we are: safe harbors of authenticity. Real bread, real people, real bakeries. It gets me out of bed in the morning.

Communities Seek Authenticity, Too

I know people in this country crave authenticity because they can get so angry when they think a pocket of "real" retail will be taken away from them. I remember several years back when Denise and Tim O'Keefe tried to open their bread store in Rockridge, a section of Oakland, California, right across the line from Berkeley. The mere suggestion that a franchise would be sowing seeds that might take root in their community brought out scores of angry Rockridgites. In their minds, Rockridge was a community, and they were determined to protect it against a godless incursion by franchising. Why? Because they knew that if they let one franchise in, others soon would follow, and suddenly Rockridge would lose what was so special about it and start to look like every other suburban community in America with miles of McDonald's and Burger Kings.

Kind and gentle souls, Tim and Denise were shocked by the reaction. They had just wanted to open a neighborhood bread store and couldn't believe groups of people they had never met before would work hard to keep them from doing it. At the same time, they sympathized. The reason they had been attracted to Great Harvest in the first place was that it allowed, even celebrated, creating something new and unique.

At the end of the day, Tim and Denise got the permission they sought and have even grown to be treasured by the residents of Rockridge for the warmness of their store and their generosity in the community, but the neighborhood's point is well taken.

It is our love of the authentic retail store that makes every one of our stores different. Some Great Harvests are long and skinny like bowling alleys. Others are short and wide with bread production spilling over into what should be their customer areas. Still others find their homes in what surely must have been old 7-Elevens. Some Great Harvests are bright and bursting with primary colors while others are plainer, like a simple Iowa farm kitchen in which you might find a mother and daughter baking bread. Some Great Harvests pulse with loud kinetic music. Others are more sedate, preferring the cool rhythms of a good jazz guitar. All are interesting because they reflect the different personalities of their owners.

I found another quote in an old newsletter from Pete in which he revels in how different each of our bakeries are:

> Every single bakery out there is a perfect reflection of its owner and staff. There are bakeries that are nothing like our bakery here in Dillon, and yet they take my breath away how beautifully they run, how beautiful they are, how completely unique. As a lover of bakeries, I see flowers growing everywhere in Great Harvest, all different colors and species. Go, try and find two great bakeries, run identically—you can't do it. On the surface, there are similarities of style. But under that surface, where things count, there's always the deeper personality of the place as totally indefinable, totally worthy of respect, and it is the people.

Which is how it should be. Businesses should be beautiful and unique. The genius of the Great Harvest system is that it produces so many flowers so consistently. When owners are free to create their own businesses, what else can they do but fashion something in their own image and in the image of their community? What else can they do but build something unique and above all interesting? There is a lesson here. No matter your work or your business, strive to include personality in everything you do. It is powerfully magnetic.

•　　•　　•

In many ways, I have grown up as a professional at Great Harvest. My first year, I was the system's newsletter editor. Later that year I was asked to visit bakeries and give owners feedback on their strengths and weaknesses. Sometime in my second year I took on the task of organizing what the system knew about how to promote our bread and our bakeries. My third year, I was asked to head up the field support department, a team responsible for buying wheat, visiting bakeries, publishing our newsletter, holding our annual convention, and marketing. A year later, Laura and Pete asked me if I would run the company day-to-day, naming me chief operating officer.

No question, Great Harvest has been good to me, using my talents to help build the company. But it has asked me to put some of my best ideas on the back burner so that I could pursue the company's goals. There are days when I wonder if a little more freedom in my life wouldn't be a good thing. On the one hand, I love the collaboration that is so much a part of working for an organization. I know my role and what is expected of me. But there are times when I wonder what it would be like to be in the driver's seat.

When Pete Wakeman writes, "Freedom has always been, and always will be, the freedom to do what you think is right without justifying it first to others," a little part of me inside sighs. What about me? I think plaintively. I justify all day long. It's my job. I read these words and I know that as good as this community has been for me, there will be a time when I will need to go my own way. One day I too will want to drink of the clear, cold waters of pure freedom. As right as Great Harvest's balance is between freedom and collaboration, it is slightly off in my own life.

It has to do with a deep desire to express my authentic self more fully. When I look at the people I most want to be like—Jerry Greenfield, Anita Roddick, Jimmy Carter after he was president, Oprah—I see authentic individuals, people who aren't afraid to be themselves, warts and all.

I've made a study of this question of authenticity in people. Why is it, I ask myself, that many people subordinate their personalities to a mass culture, becoming outlets of a big chain if you will, while a few stalwarts hold on to who they are—becoming the Moms and Pops we all love?

I think the answer is freedom and fear. When I abandon my true self it is often because I think I don't have a choice. I trick myself into thinking I can't turn off the TV, or that my tie has to match my shirt, or I that I can't change jobs, even though I know none of this is strictly true. I am scared of what would happen to me if I took these risks. Probably nothing, I think to myself, but why push it when it seems so much safer to walk down the more worn path?

The people who are the most fun are the ones who have some flavor to them, a strong identity. At the same time they are not too thought-out. While they know who they are, they are not too self-conscious or over-designed. One way we can tell this is that they have a certain lack of consistency. Press them to be consistent and they rebel. "Hey, this is just who I am." There is something unbashful about who they are, as if they are saying, "I am a person. Take notice!"

8

ATTRACTING
GREAT PEOPLE

Here in Dillon, Lisa Wagner has one of the harder jobs in the company, which, if you knew Lisa, you wouldn't think was right. A tallish, striking woman and the warmest person you'd ever want to know, her job is to decide who opens a Great Harvest and who doesn't. With thousands of people writing us for information about how to open a bakery every year, this means Lisa is busy. The worst part is that she must say "no" to so many people.

A networked company is only as strong as its members. The idea that Great Harvest owners are free to create stores with personality falls flat on its face if the people we ask to join us don't have personality in the first place. Likewise, while it might be true that owners are free to tweak the original Great Harvest concept and link with one another to produce a steady stream of innovation, none of that potential will be realized if owners don't actually take advantage of their right to experiment. This is why so many of the strongest networks are closed as opposed to open. The Massachusetts Institute of Technology, for example, is a network of free faculty and students, but it certainly wouldn't be as strong as it is if it had an open admissions policy. It limits who can be part of its group, using strong criteria to select group members. Great Harvest does the same thing, which is why Lisa's job is not just hard, but vitally important. *Great stores are always owned by great people.* When Lisa does a good job picking people to open bakeries, our job as the franchiser is easy. When we grab hold of a sour apple or two by mistake, we all end up puckering our cheeks for years. Picking our partners is as close as we come to choosing our destiny. You become the people you surround yourself with, and they become your future.

Take Scott and Sally Creevy, for example. They own the Boulder, Colorado, bakery. So wise a decision was it to pick them that if the Creevys were stock, we'd all be millionaires today. A Lansing, Michigan, ski bum looking for a way to stay in Colorado, Scott applied to us in 1983. Sally's sister, Jacque, owned the Great Harvest in Spokane and had told Sally it was a good deal. Sally says she had to talk Scott into the business, which is funny because he's a real natural. Stepping up to the plate, he just started knocking balls out of the park one after another. The Boulder bakery is one of the system's most successful, but more than that, Scott has helped us open countless new stores as an opening trainer. With others, he developed the system we use to pick locations. He served on the system's owner advisory council, and helped develop our current understanding of how best to stone mill whole-wheat flour. Then there are all the out-of-town customers who pass through the Boulder bakery's doors, fall in love with his bread, and decide to look up a bakery closer to home. Or the customers who write us and say, "I love that bakery. I want to do the same thing here in Kalamazoo. Can you help?" It is as if Scott dropped into our pond fifteen years ago, and years later we still see the ripples.

Picking Strong Owners

Lisa, with others in the company, has worked hard to define the qualities owner-candidates must have to succeed with us. They are: a good fit, financial strength, and a history of success.

Fit means would-be owners are generous, have a sincere desire to learn and an abiding love of great bread. In other words, their values are in sync with ours. The problem with fit is, if taken too far, it becomes a homogenizing force. "Fit can become synonymous with 'looks like me,' " says Lisa. "One of my jobs is to guard against that and to seek diversity in owners, because in diversity there is strength. That's why I define fit as 'sharing our way of looking at the world.' But at the same time candidates need to be at home with their individuality, happy with themselves and what they want to do. Fit, looked at this way, is not the enemy of diversity, but actually gives us permission to be more diverse."

The second thing Lisa looks for in would-be owners is *financial strength*. She explains, "We expect prospective owners to have the cash necessary to open a bakery or the ability to raise it. But we are not interested in investor-types, people with money but not the desire to be involved. We want people who intend to be present and work physically in the business."

Finally, Lisa looks for a *history of success* in candidates. "This means they have accomplished the things they wanted to do thus far in life," says Lisa. "They haven't just dreamed their dreams but have made them happen. Would-be owners don't have to be already-proven business people or 'successful' in some traditional sense of the word. Rather, they need to have passion for what they want to do and for what they have already accomplished. Passion, in my experience, is the thing that makes people want to do a good job—the hidden dynamo that fuels success."

These three key items come together in Lisa's mind to create a picture of whether or not a person is a good choice—both for us and for them. According to Lisa, "Financial strength is the low bar. Without it you just can't open a bakery. History of success tends to predict whether or not a bakery will take off, but it is fit that has the most to do with whether or not an owner is going to be happy with their choice to join us. Some people think that if the bakery is successful, they'll be happy, but that's not always true."

The lesson in all this is to understand that the screen through which members must pass before joining a community—whether it be a business, a book discussion club, or an online affinity group—strongly influences how successfully that community will work. The more clearly defined the criteria for entrance into a group, the more effectively the group can pursue its purpose.

Freely Chosen

At Great Harvest we never sell people on the virtues of joining us, feeling that the group is strengthened by its all-volunteer nature. Lisa puts it this way:

> People who have my position in other franchises are sales people. They are commissioned and try to sell the business to the prospect. When I talk with my peers in other companies, they are always talking about "closing the deal." I see myself differently. I am a provider of information. We see people who want to open a bakery as potential partners. They should be checking us out just as we should be checking them out. If it is a good fit, then we should proceed.
>
> I have two goals—one is to find good people for Great Harvest, but two is to match this opportunity with people for whom it would be a good thing. That's why I flood new people with information. I tell them all the good things about owning a bakery, but I describe the drawbacks, too. I tell them it is hard physical work, that this isn't a turnkey franchise, and that it isn't for everyone. If Great Harvest isn't the right thing for them, then I want to help them see that. My feeling is that if Great Harvest isn't good for someone, they won't be happy and if they're not happy, they will have a hard time building a successful business which, of course, affects the long term health of this company.

Lisa also describes how we as a franchise help owners succeed. She speaks about the learning community and how it operates. She also shows the reams of materials the system has produced on how to bake great bread, promote a bakery, create magnetic customer service, manage money, and grow. She tells would-be owners how we build on our size by buying ingredients as a group and how we produce marketing materials together. While creating common marketing materials may seem at odds with radical freedom, it is not. That is because we never force or even ask owners to use those materials. They are free to go their own way and in fact, many of the best marketers in the system don't use our stuff. They do their own art and promotions, teaching and leading the rest of us. Shared materials, however, are a great help for the owner who feels weak when it comes to marketing.

People are the iron from which our success has been wrought. Without excellent people, Great Harvest would be nothing but a bunch of dog-eared old recipes. But it is more than that. It is a collection of wonderfully interesting, alive people who bring to the community their passions, whims, gifts, and talents. It includes the Dillon staff, owners, and employees.

The Finest Crew Imaginable

Owners may write the lyrics to their stores, but it is their employees who sing the song. Here is how we attract and keep them. I've spoken to a lot of owners about how to hire great people, and they always say it is a catch-22. If existing employees are uninspired, owners have a terrible time finding good people and, in the end, have to settle for second best. Owners who have super crews, however—folks who rush to the counter when customers come in, and who run the store like it was their own—never have any trouble attracting other great employees. When they advertise for a position, they have a line out the door.

Why is this? Why is that some are so blessed while others go hungry?

Recently, I visited JoEllen and Rand Kunz in their West Salt Lake
bakery. We had lunch together in a little Mexican place, a couple of
miles from the store. JoEllen and Rand are known for their great crew,
so I was eager to learn their secret.

ME: What makes your store different from other non–Great
    Harvest stores here in the Valley?

RAND: People tell us we have great bread and we do, but it's
    the fun we have in here that makes this place great. It wasn't
    always that way. When we bought the store, sales were
    down. The bakery was dying a slow death. A lot of the way
    employees were treated was fear-based—do this or we will
    fire you—that sort of thing.

JoELLEN: We walked in and knew we had to change things.
    We had a run-in with the manager fairly quickly and ulti-
    mately asked her to leave. One of the first things we did was
    put some happy music on. We also knew we had to alter the
    way the store looked to let everyone know that something
    was going on, but somehow not make things so different that
    customers thought we were changing who we were. Next we
    sat down with the employees and said, "We're going to work
    hard and expect you to also. We will never ask you to do
    anything we wouldn't do ourselves and until we start making
    money. We are going to pay ourselves less than we are pay-
    ing you."

ME: If you could point to one thing that has driven your suc-
    cess since then, what would it be?

JoELLEN: Our people. That's simple. Our people are enthu-
    siastic and interested and that makes the experience of com-
    ing into the store fun and alive which keeps customers
    coming back. We have lots of people who travel long dis-

tances just to buy bread from our store because our people are so good.

ME: How do you fill your store with such good folks?

RAND: Hire for personality; we look for personality when people come in looking for work.

JOELLEN: We ask what makes them happy, to tell us about their passion.

RAND: If they can't come up with anything, we don't even bother.

JOELLEN: I always tell them this is not simply a bread store; it is a little piece of heaven. If you can do the work, if you can keep giving all day long, it will fill you up.

Rand and JoEllen are good people, and their lesson is powerful: the people we select to join our crew has a way of predicting whether or not a business will succeed or fail.

Keeping Good Employees— The Four C's

As I write this, the country is enjoying the lowest unemployment rate in thirty years. That's really saying something. Most people who want jobs, have work—with the possible exception of some people in inner cities and rural regions. This is good. The despair of the unemployed poisons the water from which we all drink. When everyone has a job, we all feel a little bit lighter, and we are much healthier as a country.

If you are a business owner, however, low unemployment means trouble. It is hard to find people to bake the bread. Some bakeries still have waiting lists for people eager to push dough for living, but most have to look for great help. As you can imagine, there is lots of talk in our system about what turns employees on. Here's the consensus.

Coolness—When I ask the people who make the dough, work the front counter, and wash the floors what they like about working at Great Harvest, they almost always say, "It's a cool place to work." What makes a store "cool"? We're not entirely sure, but we do know that the same things that draw customers in—the energy, the great bread, the happy smiles, and the genuineness—keep the employment applications pouring in.

Fairness and fun are important elements of coolness. Says Tom Cordova, a former Salt Lake City employee, "I loved working in Paul Maurer's store because he created an honest and open workplace, where people didn't talk behind each other's backs. He also worked hard to create an atmosphere where we were having fun even as we worked hard."

Compensation—Great Harvest pays people generously. In the early twenty-first century, there is one truth about compensation: everyone is in on what everyone else makes. Period. Your newest rookie knows what Burger King and Stop and Shop are paying, as well as what the woman who comes in to make cinnamon rolls at 5:00 A.M. earns. That means there is less margin of error when it comes to pay. You have to have a clear philosophy of pay, or else you will get caught in inconsistencies. Our philosophy has always been to do a survey of similar retail jobs in a neighborhood and offer fifty cents or $1.00 above the prevailing wage. Says Lee Christianson, our senior startup trainer, "We want to hire the cream of the crop. So we tell owners to pay above the going rate."

There is a similar philosophy in the franchise office. Our staff's base pay is fair (meaning average) for people doing similar jobs in the Rocky Mountain West. On top of this we pay up to twenty-five percent of base pay in profit sharing. This philosophy does two things—it allows us to attract and retain good people because our total compensation package is generous, but it also ensures that if times get tight, we are not locked into a bloated payroll. Generosity toward employees is important to us—whether it be toward bakery or franchise employees.

We don't believe in individual incentive pay, however. Conventional wisdom is that people will work harder if you hang carrots in front of them. That's true, but individual incentive pay has the effect of alienating people from their work by focusing them on the expected bonus and not the work itself. While employees need to be fairly compensated, we believe workers who see making money as their first priority will produce work that is inferior to employees who find their highest satisfaction in the work itself. We do have a generous profit-sharing program, the bonus that is awarded at year-end for meeting corporate goals. This rewards everyone for building the whole business. It helps workers pull together for the common good and lessens competition for individual recognition.

Caring—Simply being told "thank you" is still the best reward for a job well done. Caring can take forms other than praise, however. Some Great Harvest owners go out of their way to learn their employees' tastes, giving that just-right CD or book in lieu of the more empty $20 bill for a birthday or a job well done. Others try hard to see where their employees are headed after their time with Great Harvest, knowing that no retail job is forever. Owners help them get there, whether it be arranging the schedule around their classes or teaching them Quickbooks so they leave the bakery with a solid skill. We've found that helping a young person chase their dreams does not have to be expensive; it can be as simple as introducing them to a friend accomplished in the young person's chosen field of interest.

Connection—People need to feel connected to what they do. Most owners in Great Harvest work hard to create meaning in the workplace by helping their crew see what they do in the context of a larger story. Often you'll hear an owner describe the work of making bread in terms of what role it plays in the community, "We make nourishing bread that gives our customers the health and energy to lead good lives."

Owners also pride themselves on creating connections between employees. As a system we've come to understand what is already well known in the military: human beings will work harder for the respect of their peers and for the good of the group than they ever would for themselves.

One of the strongest connections owners make with employees is by encouraging them to act out of their best selves. Bonnie Johnson Alton, owner of the store in St. Paul, Minnesota, says, "We have a rule in our store: If you don't know what to do in any given situation, do whatever is the most compassionate and kind—you'll make the right choice."

Of course, the ultimate benefit of being a Great Harvest employee is the chance to own your own store. Here is where the Four C's come together in a dramatic way.

Owning the Shop

One reason JoEllen and Rand's operation is so good is that JoEllen and Rand learned the business from the ground up. They weren't always the owners. For many years they mixed the dough and waited on customers as employees at the Holladay bakery in Salt Lake City.

One of the most gratifying things I've seen in Great Harvest is the number of bakeries started and owned by former employees. This is not one of those ideas that someone in the front office thought would be good and foisted on the system. It emerged on its own like a beautiful wildflower poking out its head between two rocks. Other chains give their line people health insurance or a little stock, but increasingly Great Harvest employees are being given a chance to own their store some day. Thirty stores, or one-fifth of our system, count former employees as their owners. We've seen employees making $8 or $9 an hour work their way into full ownership of a bakery worth a quarter of a million dollars or more.

Paul Maurer—former owner of the Holladay store in Salt Lake— started it all. Tall and almost gangly, a social worker by training and a skier, Paul was known as a great baker throughout the system. His most lasting gift to the system, though, came when he decided to open a second store with Tom Cordova at 9th and 9th in Salt Lake, and then a third with John and Kim McGregor over in the West Valley.

Then he sold his first bakery to Nan and Steve Washburn and the third to Rand and JoEllen, *all former employees.*

If you think that these second stores are somehow weak cousins to their parent stores, it is not the case. Each of the stores started by Paul prospered and grew on their own, even after Paul left our system.

Tom Cordova—now an owner of the 9th and 9th store in Salt Lake City and Paul's first partner—remembers that initial experiment well.

I owned this woodworking business and employed this guy named Mark who also worked over at the Great Harvest owned by Paul Maurer. He'd always bring bread and cookies to the shop and I remember thinking they were amazing. He kept bugging me about Great Harvest. It was as if he knew this would be a good fit for me. I remember talking with Paul one day. We really hit it off so I began to work for him in the store. Neither of us was driven to make a lot of cash. I liked that in him, and the fact that he lived a balanced life and had a solid spiritual life. Although I loved the work, I'll tell you it was tough. I was thirty and had worked heavy construction before, but this was *hard* physical work. Still I enjoyed it. I liked the balance between the physical and mental parts of the business. I loved woodworking, but being alone in the shop all day was too contemplative. This had that but it also had the social side. I got to mix it up with customers and employees. Mark was right. It was a good fit.

One day I asked Paul if he ever thought about opening more stores, telling him if he were interested, I'd love to partner with him. A couple months later he told me about a good used equipment sale up in Idaho and suggested I check it out if I still wanted to open a bakery. I just grinned and said, "Hell yes!" When I saw the building at 9th and 9th for rent, I told Paul, and he put in a bid.

Many companies, particularly restaurant companies, use managers to open stores, even giving them slices from the equity pie to keep them motivated and focused. What's different about what Paul did, and about what the system has done since, is that nearly all the partnership agreements contain five-year buyout clauses. Partners, at their option, can be completely independent owners in five years. In fact, since Paul's successful experiment, the entire franchise has shifted toward encouraging so-called "insider" growth. When an owner opens a store with an employee and gives them the buyout right, the franchise waives all fees associated with the startup. We know that someone who has run a store for five years will be a great owner and is going to contribute to the system as a whole. Conversely, we discourage owners from taking on more than two stores by prohibiting ownership of more than two stores without a partner. We are clear in our heads: if we want to create stores with a Mom and Pop feel, we have to insist on a strong owner presence.

There is a generous feel to this kind of expansion in Great Harvest. Says Sally Weissman, who's built three additional stores in the Minneapolis area with partners, "We didn't open a bunch of new bakeries around our first store on Upton Avenue because we wanted to make more money. We did it to give some of our best people the same opportunity we had."

Adds her partner, Tom Amundson, "Our main goal is fill the Twin Cities with a community of bakery owners who share our philosophy of business. We'll make money through these agreements, sure, but our main goals are to create good bakeries and help our people." The lesson in this is that smart business owners need not just to provide a chance to advance, but also to provide opportunities for employees to take a crack at real freedom, which may mean some form of ownership.

•   •   •

On the drive back from Salt Lake to Dillon, I reflect on my impressions of how JoEllen and Rand conduct their business. They run a great bakery. They do a really good job of refusing to pass on the bad stuff that inevitably gets laid at their door—the grumpy customer, the late supplier, the missed promotional opportunity. They are a positive energy factory. All sorts of stuff comes in—but they only let good go out the front door. People find that attractive and go out of their way to stop by for a visit. There seems to be another lesson here: that every day we have a choice—to be a drain on those we meet or to pass on good energy. Be a source of negativity in the world or a source of light.

I wonder about myself. Too often I get wrapped up in my own little universe and pass on the negative stuff like some hot potato. Even worse I catch myself on bad coffee days actually amplifying negativity that comes my way. A friend calls to say a spouse is acting badly, and I jump all over Mary that night as if she had even the slightest thing to do with my friend's situation. Or an owner gives me a hard time for not doing a better job leading the system, and I'll turn around and let an unkind dig against that person leak out to someone here in the office.

I'd like to do better. One of JoEllen and Rand's secrets, I think as I pass Pocatello, is that they have gathered a great community of kindred souls to work with them in their bakery. These people all care about being good to one another and to the customers and help each other do that dozens of times every day. It is as if they know a basic truth: Who we hang out with is an important ingredient to who we become.

I know this has been true in my life. When I was in college, I desperately wanted to be a vegetarian but couldn't make that happen. Every time I went to the cafeteria, my self-discipline collapsed, and I grabbed a burger or a pork chop. Then one day, I had an idea: I'd join Harkness, one of the vegetarian dining cooperatives on campus. Maybe that would help. I did and it worked. There was something about being surrounded by a community of people who wanted the same thing that supported me in my choice. But there is more to this story. Harkness changed who I was in ways that were bigger than simply turning me into a four-year vegetarian. That community gave me much of what I count as my politics today. It shaped the way I view economic development, nutrition, decision-making, leadership, race and gender. Early my second year there, the group asked me to represent it on the all-campus co-op board, which got me involved in the business side of running co-ops. When I graduated and applied to the Peace Corps to become a volunteer, it was my co-op management experience that interested them, not my studies in political philosophy. That led me to Cameroon and some of the best friendships I've ever had. Then it was the Peace Corps connection that led to an introduction to Mary, who had also been a volunteer. Is it too much to say that Harkness set me on a course that ultimately gave me my kids, Valerie and Wilson, and that absent that Harkness community, I wouldn't have met my wife and partner, Mary? I don't think so. The people we hang out with, our friends and work colleagues, are who we are and who we've become.

I don't know about you, but for me freedom usually has a kind of lonely feel to it. The people who are into freedom in our culture can be loners—"Get away from me; I want to be free to do my thing. I don't want the constraints of the community put on me." It can have a negative connotation. Freedom from authority. Freedom from taxation. But there is another side to freedom. That's the "freedom-to" side. Freedom to choose. Freedom to express yourself. Freedom to associate. That's the freedom I see at work in Great Harvest. No one is here because they have to be. Everyone chose to participate in this community. They looked at this place like I looked at Harkness and said, "These people are who I want to become."

9

IT'S THE WHEAT

I've been baking and hanging around bakeries for eight years now, but amazingly, I've never been on a wheat farm. I decide to remedy that, asking Susan Downer, our wheat manager, if I can tag along on one of her trips north to wheat country.

Heading North

We take off at seven in the morning in her dusty little blue Toyota, heading north on I-15. I am excited to be out of the office and road-tripping to a part of Montana I don't know well.

We pass the high peaks of the East Pioneers to the left, then the Hogsback to the right, before climbing to the continental divide and then down into Butte. Great Harvest has a bakery in Butte, but we decide to keep moving, because Susan made an early appointment with wheat farmers, Phil and Laurie Ferda, east of Great Falls.

We climb nearly 2,000 feet up onto the Boulder Basin. The clouds hang low, frosting the trees and scattered ranches of Elk Park. The entire valley looks like the inside of an old freezer that has been left too long without defrosting.

Something Debbie Harrison Huber mentioned the other day has been rolling around in my mind. She said, "We bake the best bread in the world. I've never tasted anything better. I've never understood how anyone could eat our bread and want to go back to supermarket bread." She's right. There is something magical and really different about Great Harvest bread. The bread actually gets fan mail.

Much of this is the wheat we use. Every company has to have things that give it an advantage in the marketplace. One of those things for us is that we live in Montana and have access to some of the best wheat anywhere.

Susan, who grew up on a wheat farm outside Billings and is a Cornell agriculture graduate, is as smart as anyone about what makes great whole-wheat baking wheat. Before we hired Susan, our wheat was good but variable at best. After she had been working for about twelve months, our wheat suddenly became wonderfully consistent, resulting in great bread every time. Susan had burrowed into the science of baking and figured out what works for whole-wheat bread.

Quality

When I was first learning how to bake, I ran across a little patch of prose in our training materials. I still think it stands as a kind of credo for our bread:

> In Great Harvest, we CARE ABOUT THE QUALITY OF EACH SINGLE LOAF. We don't think much in terms of batches. We look at each loaf, and know that loaf is going to end up in someone's house, all alone, and that it won't matter to those people how good all the other bread was that day. The bakery will be judged on that loaf alone, even if 999 other perfect loaves were produced.

This is true no matter what business you are in. A reputation is built day by day and loaf by loaf.

Susan learned that top quality wheat is the first place you start if you want to produce excellent bread. Susan never contracts in advance with a single farmer for their wheat. Instead, she sees what is produced in a given year and then picks the very best wheat available. Some years a farmer might earn the premium Great Harvest pays for the best wheat, but other years his wheat might just be a little too average and then must go to the big flour mill in Great Falls or out on the long trains destined for Portland and then overseas.

And yet some farmers make the grade year in and year out. It makes me curious. How do they do it? Phil and Laurie Ferda are two such farmers. They have sold to Great Harvest for the last ten years running, and I am eager to find out why.

The Ferda Place

North of Helena we slide through the narrow Missouri River canyon passing Wolf Creek, Craig, and some of the prettiest scenery in western Montana. The mountains rise up on either side of the river, sharp and tall but rounded at the top. With the air beginning to warm and the clouds lifting, the scene reminds me of those pen-and-ink pictures of Chinese mountains with rivers down low and old Chinese men with long stringy beards in the foreground.

Then, just as quickly, we are up on the Great Falls plateau, out of the mountains and on the high plains. We swing east and climb up on the Highland bench, snake our way north to Highwood, then back east to the Ferda place.

The first thing I notice is that the Ferdas' spring wheat is already coming up. Little green shoots stand about three inches high, parting the black rich-looking soil and reaching toward the sun. Wheat is planted as far as you can see, even on furrowed ground right up next to the long drive to the house.

The Toyota swings in and finds a place across from the corral. We get out and rub the kinks from our legs, stretch, and look around. The place is beautiful and tidy. Some farms are junkyards with stacks of rotting fence poles and broken tractor parts, but not this place. The main work area is a couple of hundred yards long and maybe seventy-five yards wide. On one side are the house and farm sheds in a neat row. On the other side is the corral and rows of grain storage bins also in a neat row. A cow and at least one horse graze in a fenced area, and half a dozen chickens peck around in a pen. A balance pervades the air, as if the place hasn't been dressed up just for us but is rather the product of a well-ordered mind. Without even meeting the Ferdas, I sense this attention to order probably has a lot to do with why they are able to grow superior wheat year after year.

Phil comes walking over with a broad smile and a big handshake. He's bearded, sunburned, and glad to see us. Dressed in an old flannel shirt, Wranglers, dusty boots, a "Denny's Service and Repair" hat, and a blue bandana knotted around his neck, he seems completely at peace. Some people roll out of bed happy every day and Phil looks like one of those people. His entire face seems to smile.

The sky is blue and the sun is blazing, bouncing off the Highwood Mountains to the east and the Bearpaws and the Sweetgrass hills in the distant north. I comment on the beautiful day. Phil says he'd agree if we were going on a picnic, but he'd rather see rain. It's been dry for a while now. Which shows what I know. I ask him if this year is worse than others. He answers, "Yeah. When my dad owned this place, it seemed like we'd get these storms that would come from the north and dump spring rains on us every year. Other guys would complain and say the rain would just come over and hit us and no one else. I am not sure if that was true, but I do know we'd get spring rains real regular. I remember being cooped up in the house as a kid and driving my mom crazy. They used to call this place 'God's country.' But then the rains seemed to stop. Nineteen eighty-five was a teaching year. We never carried crop insurance until then. We used to get two cuts of alfalfa on this place, but these days I can't get one. There is no question, we're in a drought cycle right now."

Even during years when it rains a lot, the Ferda place is a dry-land operation. There isn't an irrigation system in sight. Wheat is a long grass, genetically not too distant from the native grasses that once lay across these stony plains like a blanket. Wheat loves the arid conditions found in northern Montana. Still, it needs *some* water to thrive.

We walk over to the edge of the main area and look out over the acres of little spring shoots, spreading in neat little lines for a mile in every direction. There isn't a fence in sight. I read recently that Beaverhead County, where Dillon is located, is the largest cattle-producing county in the state, which means nearly every square inch of ground in our area is fenced. Here I don't see a single strand of wire. It would only get in the way of the big equipment needed to sow and harvest all this wheat.

No fences gives the whole area an open, friendly feeling. This is antelope country. Pronghorn antelope are prairie animals and can't jump fences. Deer, on the other hand, love forests and river bottoms and are built to jump fallen trees (or fences) with ease. Antelope are built for speed. They can trot up a hill at 30 mph or across a plain at 45 mph without a second thought. Come to a fence, though, and they have to look for a downed section or wriggle under the bottom wire. Sometimes I think humans are more like antelope than we know. We need the freedom of open spaces.

Phil grew up farming this place with his dad, taking over operations in 1974 when he graduated from high school. Back then they didn't have a phone or running water. "My dad got power in the forties and we put in plumbing in 1986." Laurie—who has joined us—chuckles and adds, "It wasn't so long ago the wind blew over the outhouse, and we decided to fill in the hole and have an outhouse burning party. That was fun."

The two report on this without a hint of pride or apology. This is their life. Later when Susan and I were driving down the long lane toward the Ferda mailbox on the main road, we both marveled at how complete their lives seem in spite of its simplicity. "Imagine," said Susan, "not having power or plumbing out here during a forty-degree below zero winter. It makes our lives seem so padded and easy."

Phil's dad bought the place in the thirties. He and his father, fresh from Czechoslovakia, had homesteaded on down the road a bit, but grabbed this place when they had the chance. Back then Highwood had its own railway line and an elevator in town. These days they truck all their wheat either to Great Falls or nineteen miles up the road to Fort Benton on the Missouri.

I ask Phil what he likes best about farming. He laughs, and turns to Laurie and says, "He wants to know what I like best about farming!" Then he strokes his beard and looks me in the eye and says, "I guess I'd have to say knowing that all this is mine and that I'm my own boss. I mean, you should see some of the things I do sometimes. It is a good thing I'm not working for someone else. I'd get fired!"

I ask him to tell me the worst part of farming, feeling awkward with my canned questions—but I really do want to know. I once worked on a dairy farm for a summer, but really don't know the first thing about farming. I have a vague sense that it is part of my heritage—my dad told me that my grandfather grew up on a farm in North Carolina, but today, with only two percent of Americans farming for a living, it might as well be a foreign culture.

Phil says the worst part of farming is the weather. "It is hard having this thing over which we have no control. I can do everything right. I can buy the best seed, fertilize just right. Pick the right time to harvest, and still the weather can get me."

The Ferda place is big, but not when it comes to other farms in this part of the country. Which means they have to farm smart, and farming smart these days means getting the best price you can for your work. Phil tells me they spend extra time and attention at every stage of production: extra care during planting, close attention to fertility levels, careful harvesting in the old "seventy-seven hundred"

John Deere so there is less damage to the wheat. That and a lot of heart for what they are doing.

I look back through my notes and I'm surprised I don't have Phil telling me that he loves this place, but then that makes sense to me. Phil doesn't love this place so much as he *is* this place. With his own hands he planted those windrows around the perimeter of the main area. He remembers when the well turned alkaline and he stopped using the windmill to draw water. He built his machine shop tool by tool. "I have a degree in automotive mechanics, so the shop's probably a little better than most," he tells me. Above all, he tends this wheat as if it were one of his children, getting up early to plant before it gets too hot, harvesting from dawn to dusk to get the wheat out of the field and into the bins before the hail hits, and looking at those little green shoots and feeling their need for water as if that thirst were his own.

We thank Phil and Laurie again and give them a basket of bread from the Great Falls bakery. Laurie laughs and says, "Hey, look, Phil, bread made from your wheat." Phil just smiles, but it is a good smile, the kind a person gets when they've made the world a little bit better. We say our good-byes. It's been a good visit.

Out Visiting

Back in the Toyota, Susan and I head back to Great Falls, then up to one of the grain elevators we use. It is a facility where our suppliers clean, bag, and store our wheat. I want to say hi to Eileen Bennett and Ray Dussault. Eileen arranges for the shipping of most of our wheat and Ray is the elevator's general manager. Theirs is a good operation. They care about our wheat as much as Phil and Laurie do. I get the feeling our wheat is like an infant being carefully passed from hand to hand before it gets sent out to a bakery.

Eileen's one complaint is that our new distributor delivers wheat to owners. "I liked it better the old way," she says, "when I got to talk to your owners directly. They all seemed like real people. They always had time to visit."

Visiting. There's an idea I didn't grow up with. Growing up in suburban D.C., we didn't visit much. We might go to town and "pick up some groceries," or "get gas," or "go to the bank," but never spent much time "visiting" with the clerk in the checkout line or the gas station attendant or the bank teller. In fact, even as I write this I can feel my brain say, "Well, why would you? Didn't you have things to do?" as if "visiting" were completely synonymous with "being idle."

Here in wheat country, however, people visit. When they don't, when, like Eileen, they get treated like an order-taker by a distant distribution company, they don't like it. They feel it cheapens their lives.

Susan and I say our good-byes, thanking everyone for doing us the service of caring for our wheat, and head north to a second elevator Susan likes to use. We meet Scott Johnson—Ray's counterpart up here—and we visit. Farmers drift in to off-load their wheat, but they don't look like they are in any hurry. They joke and make fun of each other, insulting each other's ground and luck. They talk about the market. They talk about hunting. These are guys who spend all day, some seasons of the year, driving a big rig at maddeningly slow speeds across bumpy ground. Scott is the connected one—the hub at the center of the wheel. In little towns like this, you can see how a good general manager is almost like the mayor. He sets the tone. He can make things happen. He leads the way. Not by e-mail or edict, but just with simple conversation and artful little soliloquies in which he weaves a joke, a little bit of respect, a tip or two, and the latest news to create a colorful tapestry that keeps everyone coming back.

We head back to Great Falls, passing through Fort Benton. A beautiful little town on the banks of the Missouri, Fort Benton is the start of the "Breaks," a deeply rutted landscape that borders the river for hundreds of miles.

Today Fort Benton only has a couple of hundred residents, but at the turn of the century it bustled. It was here that Lewis and Clark swapped their big riverboats for canoes. Later it was the end of the line for steamboats, making it the gateway to the West for a whole generation of settlers. Susan and I spend the night at the old, but recently renovated, Grand Union Hotel. The next morning, with a red sun rising along the river, I go for a run and think about all that I have seen.

I'm impressed by the care for each step of farming which the Ferdas take—not because the world is watching, they're too remote—but simply because they want to do the best job possible out of their own integrity and pride of product. I wonder how we can keep this same pride in craft and simple friendliness in all our work whether it is on a farm, in a school, or in a large organization.

But now I can't wait to get this wheat I've been following into a bakery. So Susan and I head off for Great Falls for a visit with Pete Rysted and a look at his operation.

.   .   .

Our wheat couldn't go to a better bakery than Pete Rysted's. Pete is one of our system's best bakers and also one of our happiest owners. I am eager to find out why.

Pete and I climb up to the office he's built for himself above the bakery's garage while Susan talks downstairs with Shawn, who's baking today. There in the office, attached to the wall, is the oven door from the first Great Harvest. Pete bought the bakery in 1978, but two years ago he tore the original building down and built his own dream bakery on the same spot.

I sit down on the futon couch, asking him questions about the remodel, but what I really want to hear are climbing stories. I love mountains and drink up time with real mountaineers. Mountains are a symbol of freedom, and for me those who climb the highest peaks are like messengers from a promised land—the keepers of a special truth.

"I remember my first climb," he started. "It was Mt. Rainier in June. It wasn't the scariest or worst trip I've ever been on, but it

changed my life. It opened all sorts of doors for me. The year was
1979 and it was my first trip with real mountaineering in it—you know
snow, ice, and avalanches. We ran into bad weather and spent three
days in the clouds. Pretty soon we were cold, borderline hypothermic
even. There was high avalanche danger and we'd run out of fuel and
food. I think you could say we were not really well prepared.

"On the third day, the clouds dropped a couple of feet and suddenly it was as if we were standing on top of the world. The clouds
just spread out at our feet in every direction except for these volcanoes
all around us sticking out and keeping us company. It was like a religious experience. You know how they say people who go to the moon
come back changed forever? Well, that was what it was like for me. It
was better than being Jack and the Beanstalk. It was like walking to
heaven. Not a soul up there. I was totally addicted. I came back home
and told everyone, 'This is my calling. I'm going to be a mountaineer;
this is the meaning of my life.' "

I ask him to describe one of his worst trips. "That'd be hard. There
was the time we were out in textbook avalanche conditions, pinned
down by bad weather and whiteout conditions until we bailed during
a short break in the weather, setting off an avalanche just in front of
us as we descended the last ridge to treeline. Back at the visitor center
we were conversing with some women whose husbands were heading
up with a guide the next day. We recommended not going. We didn't
hear the news until we got home to Minnesota . . . Eleven of them
killed in an avalanche.

"Then there was the time that brought my mountaineering career
to a screaming halt. It was on Granite Peak in the Beartooths in Montana. I'd just skirted a snowfield without an ice axe and slipped. Took
a screamer, at least three hundred vertical feet on a steep snowfield.
Not bad until I hit the rocks partway down. Airborne for three cart-
wheels. Put holes in every finger of my glove liners trying to self-arrest.
More boulders at the bottom. People really bounce more than you'd
think. We were seventeen miles in. I walked out, but the legs haven't

been the same since. Of course, I wasn't seriously hurt if I can still tell the story."

I look at Pete with awe and realize now why people who know him well place special stock in the way he looks at the world. He understands risk and danger as well as the sweetness of life and hard-fought success. One of his favorite expressions about business is, "The road to success is unpaved," which means the thrill of making something good happen in this world isn't easy, even if its rewards are great.

I nod, sitting there on the sofa, and pondering what he is telling me. It is true what he is saying. Call it the way of the mountains: The path to the summit is unmarked; we must all find our own way.

10

BEING THE BEST
AT ONE THING

Mountains explain why everyone who comes to know Pete Rysted really likes him. The discipline it takes to climb big mountains produces a certain strength. All those brushes with death give him a powerful equanimity. The combination is attractive and also explains why he is such a good baker: he brings a climber's focus and attention to detail to the art of making great bread. Besides, how could any baking problem ever seem like a big deal when you've gone through what he has?

We walk down to the bakery and I notice three things at the front door. First is the outline of a wheat stalk imbedded in the concrete just to let everyone know where his loyalties lie. Second is a small plaque that says, "This building was constructed by Robinson Construction," a tip of a hat to the working women and men who helped Pete tear down the original Great Harvest and build this latest version. Third is a sign that says "No Shirt, No Shoes, No Problem!" It's all here, everything you need to know about Pete Rysted: his love of bread, his respect for people, and his genuine openness to all life has to give him.

We walk over—it's time to get to the bottom of why Pete is such a good baker. Sure, we have great recipes and Pete follows them closely, but what is it that makes his bread better than most?

A Passion for Bread

"There are no secrets," says Pete, standing in front of his oven, looking in on the bread as it rotates around on the shelves. "Baking great bread is about attention to the little things. This recipe isn't that complicated. But there are a thousand different ways to mess it up. My job is to be present to what I am doing and watch the bread closely. 'Attention to the little things' sounds easy, but you won't be able to get it unless you have an honest-to-God passion for what you are doing. This is a big deal for me. It is not just bread. It's my bread. It is about making magic. I've found, if you don't have the passion, you won't see it. I can feel when the magic isn't here, but when it is, wow!"

There is a debate in Great Harvest on whether baking bread is an art or a science. The science people say that everything in this world— and especially in the world of baking bread—can be broken down into checklists—mix your dough for ten minutes, proof for twenty-three minutes, that sort of thing. The art camp agrees that checklists are helpful, but insists there is more.

I wonder where Pete stands.

"Sure it's checklists, but unless you are paying attention—really paying attention—all the checklists in the world won't save you. I've seen a lot of bakers in my life and very few of them 'get' it. It is about being calm, sitting at the center of things, having the tools of the trade at your disposal, having your experience and then *seeing* what is in front of you and making good decisions. This sounds easy, but it isn't. I've been baking for eighteen years and I'm still learning. Everybody has their true passion or at least a strong suit. I'm good at making bread. That's because I look at every loaf and ask, 'Is this the best loaf I can make?' When I see a loaf, it's the first thing I think. I never think, 'What is the best way to sell this bread?' That's why marketing is not my strong suit but baking is. It is all about the questions you ask yourself."

This rings so true to me. We choose the things at which we will be strong. It is all about the questions we ask ourselves.

Debbie Harrison Huber, one of Dillon's best bakers and a baking teacher to our new people for close to ten years, puts it like this: "Mechanics makes good bread, but it takes passion to produce phenomenal bread. The best bakers return to the bread for all their answers. You follow the rules—that's the science—but you adjust what you are doing based on what you are seeing—that's the art. Checklists are handrails. You have to have handrails. But handrails never stifle a creative person; they help creative people be more creative."

I like the way Bonnie Johnson Alton, owner of the bakery in St. Paul, Minnesota, puts it. "Baking is a blend of science and intuition. Science helps us understand how things work together chemically; intuition helps us feel for the right texture, look for the right color and know it's right. It's kinetic, it's intuitive, it's the science *and* the art. I always teach the science to employees and give them the gift of the art. It is more than just being a technician. It's allowing the love to come in."

I think what Pete, Debbie, and Bonnie are saying is true, and not just in baking, but in all work. Being present to our work, adding our creativity, and allowing the love to come in—these make for quality.

Standing in front of the oven, listening to Pete Rysted talk about his deep attention to quality, I am reminded of a point Pete Wakeman once made in a newsletter about the balance between the need in business to make the highest quality product but at the same time to manage your time wisely. Repeating a story about Frank Perdue, a man with an unsurpassed reputation for quality in the chicken business, Pete recalls Perdue's statement: "We may be the best, sure, but the only question anybody asks here is 'Can we make it better?' " Pete goes on to write, "That story hit home. That's the only way anybody ever gets to be the best at anything. That's how Great Harvest got to be the best. The minute we even think about 'best-in-town' being good enough, we're going to lose everything we've worked for."

Pete contrasts this fanatic attention to quality with something Edwin C. Bliss, author of *Getting Things Done*, once wrote about time management. "The price of perfection is prohibitive," Pete quotes. This is because of the law of diminishing returns. As Pete points out, "The cost of that last 10% necessary to bring 90% to 100% is almost never worth paying."

The challenge is to resolve these two competing virtues: first that quality should be paramount in a business, and second that it is important to be efficient with one's time. Reconciling the two, Pete writes,

The time managers are right, when it comes to every aspect of a business, except one. There has to be one thing in any successful business, the thing that you do best, which is never ever considered "good enough." When you stop to think about it, making good bread versus making great bread is not really affected all that much by how much time you put in. Sure, maybe you hover around the oven a few more minutes. But for the most part it has much more to do with caring and attention, and how important you think it is, than with the hours you put in or how hard you work. And you can't care that way without some principles of perfection.

The bread is our thing. An 80% effort to accounting is fine. And 80% effort to promotion is fine. More than that, you reach the law of diminishing returns. But in every business, there has to be one thing that gets 100%, that sets you totally apart from everybody else who is giving it 80%. Without that, you just fall by the wayside. This isn't idealism; it's a fact of being successful in anything, but especially in business.

This is what I think Pete Rysted is trying to tell me: His obsession with the best loaf of bread isn't just about some amorphous "attention to quality," it is the key to his business success and the thing that gives meaning to his life.

Bread Fads

A reporter called a while back to ask about what she called "the bread trend flashing across the country." "Are you worried," she asked, "that the fad will pass?" I thought about what she was saying and then spoke my heart:

"Quality bread is not a fad. Great bread has been a basic part of human existence for thousands of years. Mesopotamians prided themselves on their baking skills three thousand years ago and so has every culture in every land ever since. The reason all of us think of great bread as a fad is that decent-tasting bread is new to America in the last ten or twenty years. But good bread has been with us for a long time; our grandmothers baked great bread, as did their grandmothers before them. The *fad* is bad-tasting, artificially pumped-up, unnaturally preserved bleached bread. That's the fad. During a period right after World War II, we tried the chemical-bread thing for a while. It seemed so modern, so clean, but like all fads, it is fading, and good bread is bubbling back up to the surface."

That was two years ago. Last Friday I got a call from another reporter from a bakery magazine. She asked me, "Are the high protein diets hurting you, telling people not to eat bread?" It was a good question, because many of our customers have disappeared for weeks at a time as they learn to live on meat alone. The power of these diets is that they work. I have half a dozen friends who have shed impressive amounts of weight. But they are hard on the body. Personally, I believe the experts who tell us, "Eat a balanced diet that includes healthy amounts of whole grains and get lots of exercise." And while many of these diet books say that same thing, the message mistakenly carried away from them is, "Eat less bread." I believe people will continue to eat bread—lots of it—because it is easily digestible and good for you,

especially bread, like ours, made from whole grains. I expect the next
ten years will be good to the world of whole grains. Already, there are
cancer and heart claims being made about whole grains and I expect
there will be more.

The Recipe

A day doesn't go by when someone doesn't walk into a Great Harvest
bakery and ask, "What makes this bread so good?" The answer is
pretty simple. Great Harvest uses the best wheat it can find. It never
buys wheat on "specs," but insists on hand-picking lots of wheat from
individual farmers and test-baking every lot before it is purchased.
Second, it fresh-mills its wheat in all of its stores. Just like Starbucks
showed the world that fresh-grinding coffee makes a difference in how
coffee tastes, much of what makes Great Harvest bread so good is that
our flour doesn't sit around for months in some food distribution
warehouse. It is milled daily. Third, our recipe is different. Suffice it
to say that our recipe includes the simplest, freshest ingredients. For
our most basic breads, it is nothing more than fresh-milled flour, salt,
yeast, water and something sweet. We use none of those added fats
and oils you find in store-bought breads, or the dough stabilizers or
preservatives that kill taste. These ingredients are combined in a secret
and closely guarded process that brings out the wheat's true flavor and
gives the bread its unique cakelike texture. Simply put, the right ingredients are combined in the right way. That, and the love, makes
our recipe unique. Says our wheat manager, Susan Downer, "I think
it's huge that we don't use a pre-mix or bake-off bread produced in a
commissary. We bake all our bread from scratch, fresh every day. We
are connected to what we do."

Comfort Food

Bread is the definition of comfort food. Susan's memories of growing up on a wheat farm reinforce this. "One of my earliest memories is of harvest. We'd all be working from morning to night, trying to get the wheat in. But sometime in that first week, my mother would use some of the wheat and take the time to grind it up in this little stone mill we had. Then she'd knead it and bake it into bread. We'd all sit down at the kitchen table and eat it together with apricot jam. It was her way of reminding us of what we were doing."

I've heard dozens of friends walk into a Great Harvest and say the entire experience—the warmth, the smell, seeing the bread being hand-kneaded, the taste of butter melting on hot bread—resonates with them as well, even though they have nothing in their experience that seems to relate.

Is hot bread, fresh from the oven, somehow part of our collective unconscious, a symbol of home into which we can all tap regardless of whether we have actually experienced it ourselves, or is it just that hot bread is simply delicious and we all respond viscerally and power-fully whenever we come in contact with it? Whatever the answer, for many, hot bread is linked in their minds with calming thoughts and feelings of security. Bread is the opposite of "fast food"; it is "slow food" because it takes so long and such care to produce. Time for most of us is identified strongly with love. The more time a father spends with a child, the more love they each feel. The more time it takes to fix a holiday meal, the more love the celebrants feel at the table. Maybe that is what bread is all about—calling us back to those who fed and loved us. Says Susan, "It has to do with home. Our bread is the bread you make at home. Its smell is the smell of home."

·   ·   ·

Growing up I noticed my folks, like Pete Rysted, worked on giving their whole attention to what they were doing. I remember Dad building stone walls in the backyard, the sweat collecting on his brow, his hair awry, as he focused intently on finding just the right stone to complete the puzzle. Or my mother reading books in preparation for a workshop, carefully underlining the best passages.

Maybe I inherited a little of that. Whenever I've baked—particularly in a big bakery where you are moving hundreds of loaves through the oven in a short period of time—I've noticed I fall into a kind of trance. Mark Peterson from Dillon, one of the people who taught me how to bake, calls it "the zone." When I am in the zone, not only do I hit all my marks, but I feel like I am really there—present to what I am doing.

I remember a trip I made with Tom Cordova—owner of the 9th and 9th store in Salt Lake—up to the bakery in St. Cloud, Minnesota. We were sitting in the back of a van and I asked him about baking good bread. He said, "The process of making bread is my meditation. To make good bread you have to clear your head of all the crap that weighs you down and just focus on what is happening."

I wish I could bring that same attention to the rest of my life. Sometimes I get into that meditative, completely attentive state when I'm baking bread, but it is hard to get in the zone when I'm pushing paper at the franchise or when I get home and spend time with my family. My problem is that I am always running toward something. I find it hard to slow down. I think this attentiveness requires us to relax our pace. I've read that some meditation traditions talk about "walking meditation." The idea is to export the same mindfulness you feel when you are in the zone to everything you do.

Sometimes, I feel tugged in different directions by the people I admire. I really respect Janene and Dan Centurione, who own two stores—one in Ann Arbor and the other in Birmingham outside of Detroit. These folks make things happen! There is a wonderful scrappiness about them. On the phone to Dillon they sound full of purpose, activity, and accomplishment. Whenever I spend time with them, I want to be like them.

I also admire Tom Cordova. Although he gets things done, I never get a busy feeling from him. I always sense deep waters. There is an appealing relaxed way he approaches life, a going with the flow. I don't mean to say that Dan and Janene aren't contemplative sorts. They are. It is as if they start off on a walk using their right feet while Tom leads with his left.

So which is more pronounced in me? I think both. It could be why I am having such a hard time being happy with who I am. Whenever I see an achiever, a pure achiever, there is a cleanness to their energy. It's all full-speed-ahead with them. No hesitation. That drive is something to be around—a wonder, really.

By the same token when I'm with someone who is strongly contemplative, there is purity to their energy. You can feel the strength of their practice. There is a kindness to their zone that reaches out and includes you. Combining these two paths—the contemplative and the active—is one of the main challenges in my life.

11

SMALL TOWN
GENEROSITY

My first year at Great Harvest, my boss, Hans Wendt, asked me to spend time in our little bakery here in Dillon to learn about how to work the front counter, what he called "the breadboard."

It was February, and I walked to work in my shorts even though the big flashing clock on the side of the State Bank building read seventeen below zero. It gets hot in a bakery once the oven starts turning, and there was no way I was going to get caught working in long pants. It was worth getting my knees nipped on the way to work to feel comfortable later on.

I was scheduled for a front counter shift with Janet Tatarka. Tall and striking, she looks a little like Lady Di and is as nice as the day is long. The music was cranked and Hans was pulling good-looking loaves out of the oven. Janet and I were having a fine time slicing big inch-thick slices of hot honey whole wheat for all comers.

About 11:00 in the morning a smallish, older-looking man with a big gold-and-silver rodeo buckle on his belt walked in the door.

"Geez, it's cold out there," he said, tossing his shoulders back and shaking off the weather.

"It is," I replied. "But it's toasty in here. What can I slice you today? We have Cheddar Garlic, Honey Whole Wheat, and Nine-Grain. The Nine-Grain is hot out of the oven."

"I'll try some of that there Nine-Grain," he said, taking off his cowboy hat and cradling it upside down in his hand like you might hold a kitten on its back.

"Here you go," I said as I sawed him off a big slab. "Remember, it's not quite done until you put some honey and butter on it!"

He laughed and used a broad knife to whittle off a generous shaving of butter from the one-pound block we had sitting on the breadboard. Next he hit the honey. I caught him squinting a little as he squeezed the honey bear with purpose.

That is when I made my mistake: I stood there staring at him. He looked up at me and then looked away with an odd little embarrassed expression on his face. Sort of like a small kid when you catch them licking the centers out of a stack of Oreos. He quickly ordered a loaf of Honey, smiled and said, "Back to the salt mines," his boots going *clop, clop, clop* as he walked out the door.

At this point, Janet turned to me with a gentle, understanding smile and said, "You need to turn away after you give him a slice."

I didn't understand. I'd been trying to get good at the breadboard, and you'd think after nine months of practice I would be starting to get the hang of things.

"You did a great job of being friendly and saying 'Hi' when he came in, but after you gave him a slice, you should have done something else like bagging bread. Let him enjoy the bread. If he wants anything, you'll notice it."

"Why?" I asked. Janet was—and still is—one of our top people at the breadboard, and I appreciated the fact that she was taking the time to further my education.

"You want to give the slice at the breadboard *without any expectation of return*," she explained. "We aren't giving the big free slice to cause people to *buy* the bread. We are giving it to them because we love to bake great bread and we want to share it with them. Nothing more. When you turn away after you give the slice, you are telling people you want them to enjoy the bread. That's it."

"But aren't the breadboard slices samples?" I asked.

"No, they aren't samples. They are gifts."

Generosity

That statement, in a nutshell, describes our guiding philosophy: Generosity is at the heart of Great Harvest. As Pete Wakeman likes to say, "The breadboard is the nucleus of a Great Harvest bakery. It's the place where bread quality and small-town generosity come together in one spot. The breadboard *is* Great Harvest."

Small-town generosity. The kind of generosity that comes when a neighbor bumps into you at Safeway as you are doing your weekly shopping and offers to take the kids off your hands for the afternoon, or when you live across the street from an older woman and get up a little early when it snows to help clear her walk.

Since that day seven years ago, listening to Janet, I have heard bakery owners again and again in different ways repeat her message about the meaning of the breadboard.

Eric Zenger (Ogden, Utah): "It's a liberation, a feeling that you are free to do things for other people."

Wade Edinger (Fargo, North Dakota): "It's giving with no strings attached."

Bill McKechnie (Alexandria, Virginia): "It's a spirit that brightens people's day."

Jeff Boeck (Hillsboro, Oregon): "It's the fact that people feel comfortable stopping in for a free slice with no intention of buying anything."

Pete Rysted (Great Falls, Montana): "You want to astound people, leave them scratching their heads trying to figure out how you'll ever make any money."

Jill Hall (Elm Grove, Wisconsin): "It's a way of life. It's giving away bread with no feeling of loss. A lot of people feel like you lose something. But you don't. It's giving from the heart."

And Bonnie Johnson Alton (St. Paul, Minnesota): "We are generous mostly because our product is a gift in itself. But our ability to give generous slices is also a way of nourishing and nurturing people. The hardest part is training young people to give everyone a big free slice. It is as if they want to protect me and the store. I tell them not to worry. We'll be all right."

When I speak about Great Harvest, one of the most frequent questions people ask is, "If you are a freedom franchise and everyone is encouraged to do their own thing, what ties you together?" The answer is "generosity." Honest generosity—small-town generosity—is one of our common threads. It is our soul.

Generosity and Business

The last line of the Great Harvest mission statement says, "Give generously to others." When I ask people what that means in Great Harvest, they always come back to the same phrase: "Giving without expectation of return." The other day, I was talking to Tim Hartfield, who, along with his wife, Jane, owns two bakeries in Portland, Oregon. One of their bakeries is right downtown. I asked Tim what happens when a homeless person comes in. Does he give them a big free slice? Or does the whole generosity thing break down? He laughed and said, "I think of homeless people as breadboard angels. To me they are a test to see if I am all bugged up and holding the bakery too closely, or I am truly giving without expectation of return. When you give hot fresh bread to someone you know is not going to buy anything, you know you are on the right track."

How can this be? How can we give away product *with no expectation of return* and possibly build a business?

Real generosity is powerfully attractive to people. When I say attractive, I do not mean in the manipulative sense of the word—I give you a big free slice of bread, knowing that you will then feel obligated to buy something—but in a deeper sense of the word. When we give something from the heart, it has a way of circling around and giving back especially if we don't spend too much time watching it.

Thinking about the process definitely kills it. If I stand at the bread-board, slicing big free pieces for all comers, and then start thinking to myself, "Look at me. Aren't I a good guy giving away all this bread?" people are going to see this and soon avoid the store, the spell being broken.

In this case, intention matters a lot.

Business people, if they hope to be successful, cannot just focus on profits. They have to find some way for their firms to "give without any expectation of return." When they do, they'll find their souls re-plenished and their energy restored.

Profit—Giving from Strength

Profits are the flip side of generosity. The breadboard feeds the register and the register feeds the breadboard. People in Great Harvest love working the breadboard—it reenergizes them—but don't let anyone tell you they don't enjoy working the register just about as much.

Profits are an essential part of any healthy enterprise. Profit is the thick, rich blood that carries oxygen to the body of our business. Prof-its indicate we are doing something right. Profits let us know that our neighbors are stopping by because we bake good bread, and our peo-ple are friendly and interested.

We like profit most of all because it helps us sustain ourselves and grow. Businesses that don't make money soon become puny and weak. After a while they collapse and cease serving the people around whom they were organized—customers, owners, suppliers and em-ployees. The first big squall and they're sunk.

Writes Pete Wakeman in an earlier newsletter:

I want this company to be like alfalfa, not wild oats. Alfalfa is a perennial; wild oats an annual. Both are incredibly aggressive and well-adapted plants. Either can out-compete the other, in the right environment. Wild oats sprout fast, have extremely aggressive growth, set lots of seed, and die. It can grow from a seed much faster than alfalfa, because it doesn't have to store root reserves. It's opportunistic and, in the right situation, can't be stopped. A lot of companies are like this, highly leveraged, fast lane, high growth. It's a proven success formula. But I like alfalfa. It takes its time coming up, but is constantly putting away root reserves, gaining strength which it will use next year. Our root reserves are to keep a good cash position and to spend on new research and learning, upgrading the business. Three years from now, a field of wild oats will be crowded out by the perennial, alfalfa. We'll operate the franchise like alfalfa, and not get too distracted by the wild oats if they pass us up this summer.

" 'Be loose.' 'Have fun.' 'Bake phenomenal bread . . .' 'Create strong and exciting bakeries . . .' 'Give generously to others . . .' " These are strong words. They are the words of a healthy group of people, not the words of an organization struggling to get by. Strength—in the sense of health, vigor, and self-knowledge—is the mother of all good feelings. You can't have fun unless you are feeling strong. You can't be loose either, or bake anything worth eating, or create anything very interesting, much less give generously to others if you aren't profitable. If you don't have ways of taking care of yourself, of loving yourself for who you are, how can you love and take care of others? You can't. You become resentful and eventually burn out. A business or a group must attend to its own needs by making a profit in order to have the energy to create quality and to be generous.

Great Harvest feels strongly that every store should be profitable every day, and that the franchising company should make money as well. It believes equally strongly that everyone should be as generous as they are able. The two work hand in hand.

All this may sound obvious or even trite, but it isn't. Unless you study businesses up close like we do, you may not know that lots of businesses don't like profits as we do. They make all sorts of choices that cause them to be unprofitable today so that they will be more profitable tomorrow or appreciate in value. This has become a particularly popular choice these days as startups forgo short-term profits in favor of fast growth. For some this will work as their revenues and values increase, but already we are seeing companies that are unprofitable for so long, they don't know how to break the habit. Theirs is a company culture based on running at top speed for a hundred yards. If you start talking about running a twenty-six-mile marathon instead, they just collapse and tell you they don't have anything left.

A Socially Responsible Business?

When interviewing at Great Harvest, one of the first questions I asked Laura Wakeman was, "Do you consider this a socially responsible company?" It was a throwaway question. I figured I already knew the answer.

Laura's answer shocked me. "We are not a socially responsible business like Ben and Jerry's. We don't have any company causes here. Our cause is great bread. We try to make good money selling that bread. When we say we are 'generous' in our mission statement, it doesn't mean we are giving away everything we have, or that saving a whale is our main concern. Our main concern is offering a great product. When we say we are generous, it means we encourage owners to give away lots of bread at their breadboard and to support causes *they* believe in, not causes we believe in."

"What about here in the franchise office?" I asked.

"It's the same thing," she responded. "We donate a fair amount to causes here in Beaverhead County, but mainly our generosity takes the form of paying people well. It's up to you what you do with your money. As it turns out, we tend to hire generous people, so they end up giving away money and time to things they care about. We don't want to pay people just okay so that we—the company—can throw a lot of support behind one thing. That's not freedom. Giving you the cash and letting you choose what you believe in is freedom and, to us, that is honest generosity."

. . .

For all the talk about "honest" generosity in Great Harvest, sometimes I feel I get it, that I am an honestly generous person, but other times I don't fully understand. I head up our local United Way fundraising effort and am quick to give $10 or $20 when a friend is passing the hat. But if I am truthful with myself, I have to say that sometimes I don't lead with my most generous foot. I'll take care of myself first and let generosity follow along like a happy little puppy feeding on whatever scraps are left over.

I reread that quote from Jill Hall and wonder at its meaning: "(Generosity) is giving away bread with no feeling of loss." How often can I say I do that? How often can I say I don't feel a little fear creep in as I write a check to the Women's Resource Center here in Dillon? Will I have enough to retire on? Should I be paying off our car loan first? Most days I give easily—particularly of my talents—with no expectation of return, but some days, I don't give so selflessly.

It is certainly not for lack of examples. I am literally surrounded by people who are practically saints in this department. There's Paula King, who shines when she talks about supporting her local NPR station in Lexington, Kentucky. Or Kayla, Conner, Paul Tikalsky, and Jen Mitchum in the franchise office who have a nearly boundless energy for owners and their interests. Or Kathy and Jim Minnicucci in Manchester, Connecticut, whose breadboard radiates generosity. Every day I see how honest generosity—at the breadboard or in daily work—creates a kind of halo around the giver.

I think one reason such generosity comes slowly for me is that real generosity requires faith. "What goes around, comes around," sounds good, but it runs counter to much of what we've been told throughout our lives. "When the oxygen mask drops, place it over your own mouth first before beginning to assist others." To be generous requires faith—that our own interests are tied closely to the interests of others.

Generosity, then, has to be rediscovered like a favorite book that has fallen between the bed and the wall. After years of learning that our first priority has to be protecting what's ours, generosity is a small, undeveloped muscle that only grows stronger with use as we relearn its power to brighten. As hard as it is to incorporate generosity into our lives, it is harder still to make it part of our business. Two reasons come to mind.

First, so much of commerce is gripped by fear. Fear that a competitor will do better than we. Fear that e-commerce will pass us by. Fear that my role in the organization will become obsolete. Fear that I won't be able to produce the results expected of me. And while fear motivates, it is terribly unattractive. We all know friends who shrink in terror at every blip in the marketplace or shift in their situation. It doesn't make us want to be with them. We may like them for other reasons—they are funny, or they treat us kindly—but not because of their fear. Fear turns people off.

Nowhere is this more true than in retail, where fear has a way of oozing out from behind a store-owner's desk, onto the floor, past the sinks and the oven, and up and over the front counter. I know this to be true from visiting lots of retail. When I walk into an establishment, I can feel how much fear there is as palpably as I can see cleanliness.

We can smell fear—the way an owner talks about her community or competitors, the way she prices her goods, or the way she treats little kids who pick up something fragile. Which is why love—fearlessness, if you will—is such a breath of fresh air and draws customers into stores like kids to a kitten. People just want to be around it. Generosity never lasts long in a climate of fear. It only thrives when an owner loves what she does, loves what she makes, and loves the people in her store. Generosity "works" because it is love manifest and love is strongly attractive.

The second reason generosity is so powerful is that honest generosity presupposes that we have gotten over ourselves at least a little bit. Generosity isn't about us. It is about other people. It is about seeing others in our lives not as obstacles or useful stepping-stones, but as real extensions of our lives. Martin Buber said we need to work on thinking of people as "Thou's," which I think means treating others as holy. "Ego," or our sense of self as all-important, stands in the way of our seeing the world on friendly, happy terms.

I know it is true for me. The more time I spend on the breadboard, the more I feel filled up and the more of me I have to give to the world. As it is true for professionals everywhere. I think of Valerie's new kindergarten teacher, Ms. Sampson. She is an extraordinarily nice and happy person. Did she bring that to her work? I am sure she did. Does it help that her full-time job is to dispense hugs? I bet so.

12

LEADERSHIP IN A
NETWORKED WORLD

When I was twenty, I went home to Virginia for Christmas. We opened presents in the morning and then went over to the Johansons' for eggnog around 4:00. That night I told my folks I was going to hitchhike across the United States to San Francisco, something I had been planning for a week or so. After the eggnog was finished, dad gave me a lift out to I-66, which puts him in the running for "good sport of the century."

Rides were easy to get that night. It was Christmas, after all. In a first for me, a state trooper picked me up. He was a young guy, my age, and amazingly gave me a ride for sixty miles without even the hint of a hassle.

Later that trip—east of Oklahoma City—a crazy old guy gave me a lift. All he kept saying to me was, "It's all out of control." Then he'd giggle and say it again, "No one. None of them. They have no clue. No one has any control." Now, I loved to talk to drivers—I thought of it as my payment for the ride. But this guy was too weird.

When you're thumbing, you shrug this stuff off—the drunks, the interminably lonely, the truckers on speed, and the religious nuts who would see me and lock on like some heat-seeking missile. Your only

goal is to make the miles, get out of the car okay, and then get another
ride without standing out in the cold too long, but this guy was creepy.
I was ready to split when he found his exit. Funny thing about creepy
people, though: they get to you. Stick to you like cockleburs.

Question: How to Be a Net Leader?

Some days as I sit here trying to "lead" Great Harvest, I remember
my Oklahoma friend. His gift to me was to remind me that control in
a world as complex as ours is an illusion and no more so than in a
wired, networked world. How does one lead a networked organization,
knowing that while control may be impossible, skilled leadership is
absolutely necessary?

Dilemma: Hierarchical Leadership
Is in Our Bones

Since we were kids, most of the groups in our experience have had an
authority figure at their helm. The church had its pastor, the school
its principal, the baseball team its coach. The fact that we grew up
seeing companies with all-powerful and all-knowing CEOs makes it
seem as if that's the way things ought to be.

We know that centralized authority works. The United States
would have never won World War II absent Eisenhower. He was in
charge. There was a chain of command, people knew their place, plans
were made, orders were issued, hills charged, and that's the way battles
were won. The war movies of my childhood taught me that to disobey
orders or to circumvent the chain of command was not just wrong, it
was treasonous—the highest crime in the land.

Orders and chains of command, of course, have their place—generally when stakes are high and time is short—but for much of life

they are inappropriate. Boss people around too much and they start to feel like pieces of a machine. They trundle to work in the morning, hang their coats on the hook, put their yogurts in the fridge, and do their little piece, not fully engaged. When labor is measured and managed too much, people get a hollow feeling and care less about what they do. They need to feel the joy of creation. In order to experience that, they can't be told simply to work hard, they need to be given real freedom.

Net leaders assume that everyone has a contribution to make that far exceeds their role. A leader's job in a decentralized organization is to create space for that contribution and to help set it in the context of a larger strategy.

Operating in this type of atmosphere bothers some people. They have grown dependent on the idea that people smarter and more able than themselves are running the world. Great Harvest is no exception. When things get tight, some people in our system start looking for all-knowing leadership from central "headquarters." In early 1997 when the market for bread softened, there were owners demanding Laura and Pete to "show some leadership." Pete wrote back, arguing that top-down leadership and the myth of the "omni-leader" is inappropriate for Great Harvest:

> The leaders-at-the-top metaphor causes much misunderstanding and unhappiness. Knowing the answers; having control; omniscience; omnipotence. Laura and I can pick one or two causes to champion (same as you, or anyone else) and work on those with all our hearts, for years. Meanwhile, concentrating as we are on what we most care about, EVERYTHING else is slipping around, and through, and over and under, and getting by us. We don't (and can't possibly) know 1 percent of what's happening. We don't (and can't possibly) accomplish 1/100th percent of what's being accomplished.
>
> And yet, people look for a top person who can head or control the thing. They like to identify a single charismatic mas-

cot, if they possibly can. They would like to put a face on the thing—because it's a big blurry thing, as indefinable as a cobweb. They look for that human face, expect it, want it, believe in it, in their gut, and will make it happen any way they can.

The damaging falsehood in the omni-leader metaphor is that it leads people to thinking there are solutions to problems outside of themselves. Giving responsibility over to others, depending on others for answers, blaming others for problems—that is a debilitating habit for any person to have. But it is even worse for a whole community to adopt into its very fabric this habit of looking to a single leader for answers. I can't imagine anything more cancerous, more fatally corrosive.

So, how do you run an organization if you don't want to adopt the top-down approach? Put another way, where does a networked group get its direction? Answer: From two sources—each worker seen as a leader of his or her piece of the action and also concerned for the whole, and from those who hold executive responsibility but use it in ways appropriate to the networked organization.

Answer #1:
Many Leaders Create the Whole
Through Their Gifts

At Great Harvest, I was taught very early that we are led by many people—by smart bakery owners; by Mandy Cufley, our newest employee in Dillon; by Mary Jo Johnson and Dianne Pelletier at the front desk; by Geoff Turner, the manager in Evanston; and by Laura Wakeman, our copresident. We call this the "many leaders" idea. Everyone has a voice, and each one has a highly defined sphere of influence in which they are the boss.

Great Harvest is built this way for two reasons. First, Laura and Pete Wakeman don't like the extrovert-leader thing. Their idea of a perfect workday is to sneak up the back stairs after everyone has settled into their routines, check e-mail, work on a writing or research project, slip out to Sarah's for coffee, and then maybe meet quietly with T. J. Nelson about the store in Butte or with Jim Huber on computers. When we think of big-time leader types, we almost always picture jet-hopping, meeting-loving, speech-giving whirlwinds. This is not Laura or Pete, which is one reason why a decentralized structure works well for us.

There is another reason we cultivate this idea of many leaders: It creates a stronger company. As mentioned before, when we define spheres of influence clearly, and create ways for people to talk, listen and learn from each other, we learn faster and create more interesting innovation as a group.

Answer #2:
Executives Use a New Style of Leadership

In addition to the leadership each person brings to a networked or-ganization, nets need a person or persons vested with executive re-sponsibility for the whole. There is much discussion these days on the nature and form of that responsibility. In some ways it is easier to define in terms of what it is not. It is not command and control. But what is it? For eight years, I have been studying the way Laura and Pete give direction to Great Harvest, eager to abstract their style into something I could define, hold, and copy. I have come to see six func-tions as key. Laura and Pete design the whole, paint the promise, set norms, create a culture, balance the network, and participate fully. Let's take a look at these.

Design the Whole

A net leader is the architect of the whole. Human networks, particularly in business, do not emerge on their own. They are created. One of the main things a leader does is define the group and then build the infrastructure of sharing—the wires that connect the computers together, the intranets, the conventions, and the cross-travel trips. Networks of people working in common purpose create a kind of super-intelligence that creates competitive advantage, but first someone has to envision and then build the net, and that's the leader's job.

In Great Harvest, that was Pete's role. He was the one who first imported the language of biology into the company, speaking of how we could link ourselves together and become a self-directing, self-adapting organism, and it was Pete who insisted on defining separate, equal and autonomous spheres of influence,

Bill McKechnie owns the store in Alexandria, Virginia. Call him up and ask him who is in charge of his store and he will say, "I am." He'll be right, too. If he wants to install blue lights in his ceiling tomorrow, have his employees all wear red, and dye his bread green, it's one hundred percent his call. The same goes for Bill's neighbor in Rockville, Maryland, Dan Gottfredson. Dan can call Bill for advice. Bill can call Dan, but they are talking as equals. Each is free to do what they want. The same is true for employees in the franchise office. Jen Giem is in charge of our books, Stefan Fromm the development of store software, and Tiffeny Millbourn our outside communications. Each is in control of their corner of the business. Laura or Pete don't tell Bill, Dan, Jen, Stefan, or Tiffeny what to do, but it was Laura and Pete's vision in the first place that created the boundaries that enable each of these to be genuine leaders in their own right.

Paint the Promise

The second critical role a leader plays in a networked organization is to paint a picture of the group's promise. Much has been written on

the need for leaders to articulate a vision for their groups by describing
the organization's mission, values and strategy. In a networked organization a leader has an additional responsibility—to describe why the
group's networked nature is an important part of reaching its goals.

Laura and Pete's vision is of a learning community and how it
creates authenticity and innovation in our business. While they clearly
talk about organizational goals—that as a system we want to be known
for our whole-wheat bread and friendly stores—they also describe why
doing this as a webbed, richly cross-linked community is advanta-
geous.

In an e-mail to the system Pete reminds us again of how our networked nature produces innovation and creativity:

> A strong distributed system re-invents the wheel in ten places
> at once, then after a while, looks up from its work and compares
> wheels. I say, contradict frequently, enjoy, promote, celebrate
> wildly conflicting signals. One harmonious hum eventually
> emerges. Let people scatter off in all directions on a search; as
> soon as the best answers are found, they gain converts, who
> teach new converts, and soon a chaotic scattered mess gets
> aligned in a stampede toward a single point.

Pete needs to do this periodically because people in our system forget
that all this absence of centralized direction is intentional and for good
reason.

At times Laura and Pete struggle to maintain their balance as store
owners argue against their vision of radical decentralization. Just as
some want Laura and Pete to assume an Eisenhower role in the company, others wish just as strongly they would step out of the way.
These voices urge us to make corporate decisions by consensus.

A love of bold, *individually made* decisions, however, is a hallmark
of Great Harvest. Before joining Great Harvest, I worked for a couple
of cooperative businesses, a student housing and dining cooperative
in college, and a palm oil buying cooperative overseas. I also sat on

the boards of a book co-op and a food co-op. In these settings I developed a love of consensus-style decision making.

With co-ops and now at Great Harvest, I've learned that decisions made by groups of people are almost always fairer and better thought out, but decisions made by individuals are more interesting, innovative, and bold.

Several years back, Pete wrote a newsletter piece in which he quoted Anita Roddick, founder of The Body Shop. In her book *Body and Soul*, she wrote:

> To be a success in business
> Be daring
> Be first
> Be different.

Pete was reminding us why we should not run our business by consensus, but should instead always give groups of one or two people lots of room to make quirky, less than fully rational, even downright stupid (or so says the larger group) decisions. Only then are markets created. If you establish lots of spheres of influence and network everyone together, you create excitement and boldness without sacrificing quick learning or, importantly, ways for people to feel like they can participate. There is a role for consensus but it is after lots of people have followed their hunches, free from having to justify their ideas in front of some council. Elected boards of directors are almost never daring or different and consequently are rarely first.

As Laura Wakeman says, "No one thought we were thinking very clearly when we opened a little whole-wheat bread bakery in the middle of a ranching town in the mid-seventies. But we did and it worked out pretty well." Individuals take risks. Groups rarely do.

Networked organizations have advantages and disadvantages. They are good at producing creative, interesting, and appropriate solutions to problems. They are bad at producing these solutions efficiently, given all the intentional redundancy. The networked model is better suited to companies where quality concerns are paramount and where costs or time-to-market are not the most important values. That's why it works so well in Great Harvest.

Set Norms

One of the things Laura and Pete have done most successfully as they lead Great Harvest is to model and highlight norms for the operation. From the beginning, for example, they have pushed for openness in Great Harvest. This is one of the few requirements written into the contract that binds franchisees with the whole. Everyone in the system promises to be completely open with their insights related to the business and the innovations they develop. Our strategy of being perfectly free, connecting ourselves together, and sharing what we have learned wouldn't work if people held their thoughts and discoveries close to the chest. It only works because owners enter into the club, understanding there is only one rule that governs us all: We all share openly what we develop. It cannot be otherwise. Year after year owners help each other in ways that defy simple business logic which says that an entrepreneur's time is limited and should be conserved. They call each other with good recipes, let each other see their numbers, and share what they know at new store openings.

Another norm Laura and Pete have set for the community is an insistence on written agreements. At Great Harvest, we write down all of our agreements—promises to guarantee royalty rates, agreements to pay fees over time, commitments to provide startup services. This helps everyone keep clear about expectations. Promises, to us, are like fence lines keeping our little circles of autonomy separate. It is a practice that runs counter to what you might expect. Often in companies that emphasize shared understandings and quality in people, there is the thought that we ought to trust each other and "keep things on a handshake." Laura and Pete have led us in a different direction. They believe the more you emphasize freedom and the absolute right of people to make their own decisions, the more you need to be crystal clear when you make agreements with one another.

Create a Culture

Much has been written on the importance of culture to a company. The organization is successful insofar as its culture—its values and mores—is aligned with its mission. I see that at work in Great Harvest. The web of information, sharing, and support that connects franchise owners together is reinforced by the culture Laura and Pete have worked to establish for the whole. Newsletters were an important part of creating that culture, particularly in the early days. Laura and Pete were the inner voice of the system—expressing its hopes, its trials, and above all, its values. We have seen an example of this in the steady emphasis Laura and Pete have placed on a love of learning in the franchise. For them, learning is one of the key elements of a well-lived life and a central part of the learning-and-innovation strategy. I know it has rubbed off on me. Here is a piece I wrote recently describing how our system is better and different because it allows for "just in time learning."

> One reason the networked future is so exciting for me is that it turns on its head the way we have traditionally learned. Instead of learning when it is convenient for the teacher, we get to learn when it best suits us. Hans Wendt, who owns the Bellingham, Washington, bakery with his wife René, calls this "just in time learning." He explains that when we were in school, we were told where and when to sit and also, importantly, what we were going to learn that day. Kids don't always respond well to that. Oddly, he notes, most company managers forget how stiff and bored they felt when they had Spanish II force-fed down their throats, conducting trainings when it makes sense for them not when it is convenient for their trainees. Good schools follow, to some extent, kids' natural enthusiasms, capitalizing

on the energy they bring to those loves. Networked access to information, suggests Hans, functions like a good school, allowing bakery owners to log on and find out what they need *precisely* when they need it most. An owner remembers there was an extranet discussion on how to clean the gas jets in their oven a while back. At the time, however, they didn't pay much attention to it. Now when their oven is acting badly, they log on and are suddenly able to find the information they need.

The fact that I would write this piece to our system, as opposed to an essay on return-on-investment, was a choice, one that I made because for years Laura and Pete have been telling us that they believe a networked organization should be a *learning organization*. A company culture is the thousands of little decisions a leader makes to emphasize one way of doing business over another reflected throughout that organization over time by the actions of others. A leader's job is to understand this culture-creating power and to use it to further the goals of the group.

Balance the Network

Laura and Pete think a lot about the nature of our network, its size and the way people are connected together. It is their job to maintain the network and fine-tune its operation.

A good example of this is the question of size. On the one hand getting bigger is good for the whole—more connections means more learning and adaptation—but on the other hand, including everyone—every counter person and every kneader—in the learning community is not necessarily good. For this reason, Laura and Pete have led us toward growth, but also toward recognizing the local bakery as the main unit of our network.

Kevin Kelly, editor of *Wired* magazine, has argued in his book, *New Rules for the New Economy*, that as networks grow arithmetically, their usefulness grows exponentially. Ten years ago the Internet existed but wasn't very useful. Today, with virtually every organization hosting a page, you don't have to wonder if you can find information on the Net; you just log on and use it. The same is true in a net-company like Great Harvest. The more "nodes" on the network, the more connections, the more the chances are that if you have a question someone out there will have an answer. For this reason, Laura and Pete have always embraced growth as a way to strengthen the usefulness of the learning community.

By that logic, we should push for more bakeries, and for *everyone* in our community to get connected, each employee of every store, both spouses who own the bakery, and all Dillon employees. But we don't. While every employee is welcome to join in the fray, there seems to be a virtue in having one owner in each bakery serve as a kind of ambassador to the whole system on behalf of their own bakery-based learning community.

Tom Petzinger, former columnist with the *Wall Street Journal* and author of *The New Pioneers*, calls this the "sweet spot" between order and chaos. Too few "nodes" and you approach perfect order. Too many nodes and you have chaos. Stuart Kauffman, the network theorist and author of *At Home in the Universe*, goes further, arguing that even if you could wire everyone together, you wouldn't want to, writing, "The coevolving system lies at a phase transition between order and chaos." It is Laura and Pete who lead us to authors like Petzinger and Kauffman and who urge us to balance efficiency and creativity. Great Harvest is an adaptive net, writes Pete, but we are "a sparsely connected *clumpy* net," meaning that while we are connected, we are most often connected bakery to bakery and not every person to every person.

Closely related to this issue of scale and the relative size and nature of the units connected together, is the question of how many connections each individual should maintain.

Everyone knows the problem of being over-connected, of walking into the office, logging on and seeing 200 messages on our screen. Over-connection causes the learning community to bind up. Laura and Pete counsel owners—based on observing what works and what doesn't in our system—not to over-connect, but instead to make five or six friends in the system and have faith that the system will "work"—that good ideas will jump from owner to owner and quickly make their way to your little five-person net.

As leaders, they talk about the dangers of being over-connected as well as the perils of being under-connected, arguing that if you talk to too many people, e-mail too much, and constantly travel, you will probably have lots of ideas for your bakery, but won't have the time to actually implement any of them.

At the same time, they warn against being under-connected as well. We see this every once in a while in owners who never call anyone, refuse field representative visits, don't go to conventions, and aren't online. They might prosper for a while, but inevitably they grow myopic and atrophy. "Stay connected," Laura and Pete tell the system.

Laura and Pete consider it their job to be students of the whole, to report their findings to members of the group, and to give feedback on how the net is or is not working.

The lesson is clear: A leader's job is not just to design and create the net, but to worry over its performance like a kid hovering over his car on Pinewood Derby night.

Participate Fully

As leaders, Laura and Pete have certain meta-responsibilities for the whole, but they also feel part of their job is to have causes and to push them just as anyone else in the system would have things they want to advance. Here's Pete Wakeman again, talking about what he feels his job as copresident is:

> I'm thinking a case can be made for SOMEBODY in the company, somebody high up, being IN LOVE with their work, tearing into projects that truly get them excited.

So I do what I love and ignore what others feel I "should" do. Just Say NO, and people will find some other way to get help, somehow.

I'm a helper myself, of course, but only sometimes. The truth is, I have some of the best connections, and access to some of the best lever points in the net. I'm versatile, and know a lot, and see patterns others miss, spot opportunities others aren't primed to see, can even produce a small amount of magic. I handle flow well. But still, I'm just a node, blind to much of the whole, limited in the number of signals I receive, and able to pass ideas along piecemeal and inaccurately. To make big things happen, I can only watch for forces already aligned in my vicinity and assist them.

It's appropriate to feel the energy flow through me, its power and elegance, and to amplify or modify what it already wants. It's appropriate to feel excitement, to move quickly, to be greedy for ideas, hungry to learn, and to feel my power. That's pleasure, what I'm made for.

But it's bogus to pretend to be at some top, or in some kind of ultimate control. Power, flow, energy, creativity, leverage: yes. But hard linkages, accountability, predictable effect, accurate steering: no. I love to play and I love my job. I have a role and I love my role. But I more respond (hopefully, with grace and alignment) than influence. The network of connections teaches me, informs me, hints to me of directions to go, asks my assistance and commitment to what it already knows it wants, or needs.

The beautiful part is, I can lean on the thing, float in it. Everybody can. Listen: You already know what will advance its causes. Be free, because that's how you're most useful to it. Have fun, because that's the way you let love pass through, make love travel back around. Never judge, never allow a bad day, and the energy will go quickly where it should. Enjoy, just enjoy, like a dolphin enjoys current and wave, or a seagull updraft and wing. I'm built for it, trained for it, in love with it, into it, part of it. Escape to freedom, every moment, every day; hear the hum and the rhythm as clear as clear music, but be blind to distorted mirrors placed around you by others, and deaf to every well-intended pronouncement of a false model built from false assumptions.

As I study the way Laura and Pete lead Great Harvest, I notice two things. First, how profoundly uncomfortable it makes some people in our system for the pair not to assume the role of all-knowing bosses. But I also notice how much more fun they seem to be having than other CEO-types I've met who seemed burdened by the feeling that their job is to work their will on their companies. I have enormous respect for the net leadership Laura and Pete offer. It is inspiring and full of experimentation. They and other leaders of net organizations are taking a stab at a first iteration of what may become a new paradigm for leadership.

Increasingly, however, I wonder how I fit into the scheme of things.

· · ·

A net is an interesting metaphor. It suggests all parts of the whole are networked with each other, creating powerful webs of interconnectivity. But there is a dark side to all this communication as well. Fish get caught in nets.

Being in a highly networked organization has its thrills—it's fun to make long-distance friends and to learn what they are up to—but it creates real unease for those on the inside, particularly would-be leaders who generally have lifetimes of Ego to overcome before they can be at all useful in this brave new world.

Where am I in all this? I'm not as sure as I used to be. I want my insecurities calmed by status or position, but it isn't happening. I want to be effective but can't figure out how to do it. What I'd really like, though, is to be able to put on Pete's good attitude like I put on a shirt in the morning.

What's stopping me? What's got me addicted to this idea that I need take responsibility for the whole? I think it has to be ego to start with. I have a pretty good self-image, but it is not so robust that I don't suffer stabs of doubt. I attempt to counterbalance that fear by asserting myself awkwardly. And of course it doesn't really work. Still I try to look confident, stand up straight, and issue "direction" where there is confusion.

I think it is a failure to commit. To love what you do, to be fully present to your work, you have to commit to that work and sometimes I find commitment like this hard. I don't totally blame myself. The curse of living today is not the absence of opportunity, it is that of having too many choices. There is so much we can do; it's hard to decide sometimes. How many times have you heard a friend say, "I don't know what I want to do." They're not worried about whether there is anything they can do. They are freaking out because there are lots of things they could do and they don't know which one will make them happy.

In a low moment a couple of years ago, I made a list.

Things I could do:

- Buy a business in Bozeman
- Run this one
- Do development work overseas
- Become a columnist
- Write a book about what turns employees on at work
- Speak for a living
- Volunteer with an inner-city entrepreneurship program
- Create a venture talent company
- Run for political office

The list went on and on. I kept adding things I could do or thought I might like to do. And that's just for me; your list is completely different. Some people don't think their list is very long, but that is only because they are not being honest with themselves about how really free they are. They could quit their job. They could move. They could leave their spouse. They could go back to school. They could do a lot of things.

All this choice breeds confusion. "What to do?" we ask ourselves. The magazine *Fast Company* says we are all "free agents," and indeed we are, but it's work being a free agent. It's work constantly inventing and reinventing who you are. It is the work of making decisions and committing.

I spoke about this recently with owners Rand and JoEllen Kunz, whom we met earlier. I asked Rand how he was doing, and he surprised me by saying, "Life is good, but that's a recent development. A couple of years ago I began to burn out. I've been at this eleven years. At the time, I would have sold this store for a buck. It was a mid-life crisis. I was miserable, tired, and out of shape—my doctor told me that I was fifty pounds too heavy. A bunch of employees left because I pushed the line too hard. The store suffered. It was a karma thing."

JoEllen nodded her head in agreement. "Rand was dragging the store around like dead weight. What I told Rand was, 'Get in there with all your heart and soul or get out.' "

"I was one of those guys who likes to keep his options open," volunteered Rand, "and it was making me miserable."

Suddenly, I nodded my head. Rand was reading my mind. JoEllen said, "Until you cut your options and tell yourself, 'This is what I am going to do,' the business suffers from your lack of attention."

She's right. You have to commit. Rand summed it up: "It's like marriage. Anyone who gets married, but keeps looking, makes themselves unhappy. Today, I've said, 'This store is what I do. It is who I am. I'm going to make it great.' "

I want to make that same commitment to what I do, but I need help in thinking it through. It feels like it would be useful to talk all this out with someone older and wiser who would reflect with me on these questions I have—that mentor I was talking about earlier.

13

COMMITTING

It's June, just about a year ago, and I'm at Papa T's, Great Harvest's living room. We take almost all of our guests there for a beer and a few games of pool. To celebrate the opening of every tenth store, we hold a company pizza and beer night, and we always have them at Papa T's.

Papa T's is probably one of the best examples of a truly Montana phenomenon: the family bar. Where I grew up, kids didn't go to bars—you know, places where whiskey was served—but in Montana the rows of liquor stacked three high share space with quarter arcades and a carousel with three mice. Kids are not simply tolerated here, they're welcomed. When out-of-town teams come to Dillon to play the Beavers, their coaches almost always take them to Papa T's, where they eat pepperoni pizzas and drink pop right alongside the old guys at the bar taking their medicine.

I'm here because I've finally decided to act on this idea of mine that I should find a mentor. I've never sought Pete Wakeman out before on personal stuff. But my general feeling of panic about who I am and what I am supposed to be doing with my life, however, has finally driven me to invite him to Papa T's.

I've always felt close to Pete. This isn't so much because we talk much or do anything together. Most guys talk sports or politics or go fishing or hiking together and find friendship in these shared experiences. Pete and I don't do any of these things. It is as if our closeness were genetic, like he and I were fashioned from clay found by the side of the same river.

Here is a guy I really admire. I mean, if I could have his life, that's what I'd like, right? Owns his own business. Three months every summer, hiking in exotic locales. A great writer. A loving relationship with his wife and kids. Fit, smart, high and happy. I could do worse.

Pete walks in, gives me a wide smile, and then sits down. We order a couple of Taddy Porters—the thicker and blacker the beer, the more Pete likes it. Which goes for me too.

We gossip about the business for a while before I cut to the chase.

"Pete, sometimes I feel a little lost. I know I come off looking self-assured and strong, but it is a façade. I just wish I had someone I could talk with, to ask a few questions of. I think they call that kind of person a mentor."

I don't think this is what he is expecting, because he looks a bit taken aback. He nods slowly and orders us a couple of more beers.

I must look jumpy at this point. I've set up the conversation so that the words, "Sure, Tom, I'd love to help you," are about the only possible ones that will avoid total embarrassment on my part. Suddenly it doesn't look like this is what will happen.

"I feel like I want a teacher and am ready to learn. One of the best ways to grow is to learn from someone you respect. I really like the way you have your life put together, so I thought we might talk about how you do it."

Pete surprises me by looking at me with real interest and responding, "Tom, sometimes I think of you almost like a little brother. We think alike on a lot of things. But I can't do what you are asking. I could never be a mentor."

I don't know what to say. Neither does he, really. When I lived in Cameroon, they always "burnt fowl" at special occasions. Instead of cutting off the chicken's head, chopping it up and roasting the pieces over a grill, they would hold a live chicken by the feet, stick its head in a hot fire and "burn" it until all that was left was a char-blackened head—brains, eyeballs and beak all fused into one. Then they'd roast the rest of the chicken before dividing it up.

That's pretty much how I feel sitting there at Papa T's.

•   •   •

But it gets worse.

A few days later, Laura Wakeman stops by to talk.

Now, let me be completely honest before I go on. I hadn't been very nice to Laura for the previous few months. Little things—the barbs we pass off as innocent, but if taken together they definitely suggest a pattern. I'd point out where she had gotten some facts wrong in front of our advisory council, or I'd snipe about how people make more at other franchising companies. Little jabs that I fooled myself into thinking she didn't notice. It was almost like a game. I'd feel frustrated, take a swipe, feel better, and figure she wasn't any wiser. Well, I was wrong. Of course.

The storm breaks just before Laura and Pete head off for the summer. Laura comes into my office and asks if she can see me later in the day.

I love to bow hunt and know from a lot of time spent in the woods that deer—especially whitetail deer—have a sixth sense when it comes to danger, especially a lead doe. It's not just that they have vision many times more powerful than ours or noses that can smell a stray scent a mile off, it's that these senses have a sort of intelligence about them. Deer can weed out unimportant sounds and zero right in on a dangerous sound, a leaf being rustled in a way a squirrel wouldn't, a set of footfalls that comes in punctuated pairs and not the more normal sets of four. They can even distinguish between the sound a predator makes and less threatening sounds, even if the latter is much louder. How many times have I seen a group of twenty or thirty deer feeding calmly while humans change irrigation pipe in an alfalfa field a few hundred yards away, only to watch the deer shy and move on as a coyote creeps in from a much greater distance?

When Laura stops by and asks to talk, my ears immediately perk up. There is nothing in her voice or in the calm, pleasant way she comes in to ask for a meeting that suggests a problem. But I know it is there. I am in trouble—bigger trouble than I've ever been in before.

Ten minutes later I walk down to confirm what I already know. "Everything all right, Laura?" She says it is, but I can see it isn't. I've fired people, and I know the fact that she wants to meet at 4:00 is a bad sign.

There is nothing you can do in situations like this but wait. Sort of like when Mom used to say, "I've had it. I'm going to let your father deal with you." So I cool my heels for the rest of the day.

How had it come to this? I wonder. I'm supposed to be good with people, able to read folks and back off when I'm pushing too hard. Yet here I am, waiting. Waiting for what is sure to be a bad talk.

When the appointed hour comes, we head into the big conference room. She sits down and begins to read from typed notes. "Tom," she intones, "I can't live like this. I cannot have my chief operating officer treating me this way. It has to stop. I feel like you don't want to be here and are picking on me instead of dealing with whatever is eating you. . . ."

Ouch! Sometimes words can really hurt, especially when they are true. This does not look good. I feel like a racecar driver hitting the wall, and I'm scared.

"I need a leader, someone to be positive about me and this company. If you can't do this . . ."

I feel my throat tightening up.

". . . I'll have to find someone else . . . I need someone who is going to support me in public and not take little pot shots because they can't make up their mind about whether they want to stay or go. . . ."

I would say something, but the words won't come. Also, I know if I speak, I'll start crying, and I'm not particularly keen on doing that just now. Finally, I choke out a response: "Laura, I don't want to be fired. I love working here."

Exactly twelve seconds before my head explodes from guilt and anger and all manner of suicidal thought, she says, "Tom, I am not going to fire you. I just want you to choose. Do you want to be here or do you want to leave? If you want to leave, I will feel sorry. You are very good for this company and we love having you here, but I won't get in your way. If you want to stay, fine, but I need to have you change. You need to make a choice."

Indeed.

Laura and Pete leave for the summer a week later, off to Ecuador to hike with their daughters. Which, at least, gives me time to think.

At first there is just anger. I am angry with Pete. Why won't he help me? Why can't I get a hand up like other people? One theme I see over and over in the biographies I read is that of an older person reaching out to help someone younger find their way or make the right connection. What's up with the "No, I can't help you?"

I'm running a lot this summer, and I find myself using the miles to sweat out all the poisonous thoughts. Why don't the Wakemans appreciate me? I've done a lot for their company. My fingerprints are on nearly every important project we've undertaken over the last five years. For this I get rebuffed at Papa T's and taken into the big conference room and knocked down a notch by Laura?

I'm done, I think. That's it. I'm out of here. They can take their self-centered ways and take a hike because I deserve better.

I go on like this for more than a month. I'm training for a twenty-mile-high altitude trail run called the "Bridger Ridge Run," and slowly all the miles begin to mend my mood. Mile by mile they begin to beat me into a higher place. By August, I am beginning to see Laura and Pete in slightly mellower terms. They aren't bad people. They are just trying to build a good company and live a good life. Nothing more.

Since I was a kid growing up in Virginia, I've been transfixed by the sight of dandelions pushing their way up through cracks in cement sidewalks. It's such a portrait of will. Truth over resistance. Once I get to the place where I can see Laura and Pete as basically good people, it is only a matter of time before my mind is open even more, and I begin to see they might be trying to teach me something.

Could it be (*no!*) that Laura was right in at least one way? That my outsized needs for affirmation are driving my dissatisfaction more than, say, this place? Well, maybe.

Could it be that Pete in refusing to help "show me the way" is in fact trying to head me in a good direction?

More miles and more contemplation and I began to see they are acting in their own way out of love. I'm out doing a run around Erb's pond when I have a breakthrough of sorts. I'm in a good space. The Erb pond run is beautiful. There are never any people. It gets me off the road to where the grass is bent over and birds chase each other like kids on a summer evening. It is hard to feel too fearful in this place.

Could it be, I think to myself, that Laura is my JoEllen? "You need to commit," she said. "You'll be happier that way." Commit or leave because being half-here is like not being here at all. She's right. I do have to choose. I'll be happier.

So I do. I climb the cattle fence out onto the road back to town and I decide to stay—to recommit myself to this thing called Great Harvest and to include it in my life, as fully as I can. Then I feel something I haven't felt in months. I feel good because I feel free. Choosing always does that for me.

Understanding Pete's gift to me is harder. It takes a long spacey run, about twenty miles out to the talc plant and back, before I begin to see his seeming refusal as a kind of *koan*. *Koans* are little Zen riddles that have no real answers but that cause us to look past them to some larger truth. They're deceivingly simple little questions like, "What is your face before your parents' birth?" or, "What is the sound of one hand clapping?"

Shibayama, a modern Zen master, explains the work of a *koan*:

Suppose here is a completely blind man who trudges along leaning on his stick and depending on his intuition. The role of the *koan* is mercilessly to take the stick away from him and to push him down after turning him around. Now the blind man has lost his sole support and intuition and will not know where to go or how to proceed. He will be thrown into the abyss of despair. In this same way, the *koan* will mercilessly take away all our intellect and knowledge. In short, the role of the *koan* is not to lead us to *satori* (enlightenment) easily, but on the contrary to make us lose our way and drive us to despair.

Could it be that Pete has given me a *koan*? I ask him, "Will you help me find the way?" He says, "No!" My sole support harshly taken away, my job is to contemplate its meaning.

The best thing about long-distance running is that you lose a sense of yourself. You just run and run, the sound of your footfalls deadening thought until you're just *there*—running. The transcendence doesn't come quickly or even all at once, but suddenly it is mile fourteen and then it's mile sixteen and you realize you haven't noticed the passing of time at all. You've just been looking at the beautiful ways the cornflowers crowd the fence line and the antelope buck stands off to the right, steady and proud.

Could it be that Pete is telling me that he is a seeker too—that none of us can show each other "the way"? Could it be that he knows that "the way" morphs into something ugly and strange when we try to teach it to others? That it is something each of us must commit to discovering for ourselves? That its very nature is better expressed in changes to who we are than in words?

I think I'm getting a glimmer of something—and it is my discovery, too. Not his.

A couple of weeks pass—the Wakemans are almost back from the summer—and I'm starting to feel a little easier about Pete. He's just a guy, muddling through, like me. The lessons he has to teach me are there to see, not covered or hidden in the back room. All I need to do is watch and pay attention. There's no need to put pressure on him to cough up the truth. Whatever he has to offer will be right there in plain sight.

Which, as it turned out, meant that I was ready—ready to see the truth of something Pete had written thirteen years ago. Something called "Newsletter #46."

14

NEWSLETTER #46
JULY 1987

"Lessons from Salt Lake"

Dear Great Harvest Owners:

The Salt Lake City bakery is two years old now. By several important measures it is the most successful bakery we have ever helped start. About a year ago Laura and I began to realize that Salt Lake is a brand-new phenomenon, something that we can't explain with our old models. The principle that is driving Salt Lake's success will probably surprise you as much as it did us. I'll start with the simple facts, then move on to the models that we believe explain the facts. I'll warn you right now that this newsletter might require all of the open-mindedness that you can muster. But I also want to state, right here at the beginning, that this is brand new material which we believe can benefit the system, and each of the bakeries in it, as much or more than anything else we've ever put in a newsletter.

The Facts

In the history of Great Harvest, only a few bakeries classify in our minds as "phenomena." Great Falls was of course the first. Laura and I can still remember the line stretching from our front door all the way down the block, the people patiently waiting for our doors to open, then selling all of our bread in less than an hour. Vic and Linda's bakery in Kansas City was the next; our first proof that we could "hit the big time" in big cities. And of course Minneapolis; still the undisputed leader of gross sales. Laura and I trained Tom and Sally ourselves, over four years ago. The day we opened the doors we knew we were in trouble. I remember being frankly worried about the location, in a side residential neighborhood with very little foot traffic, and quietly incredulous on that first day when the people came out of the woodwork. I think every new bakery since then has traveled to Minneapolis prior to picking their location, trying each in their own way to figure out what makes them "Minneapolis."

But just as Vic and Linda had to hand the crown over to Tom and Sally, now it's Paul's turn to take it. Minneapolis still holds the record for gross sales: a brand new record as a matter of fact, $42,043, set just last month. But in March, the month of Paul's second anniversary, he did $36,125 in gross sales, almost pure retail, almost pure bread. Tom and Sally's gross sales on their second anniversary of business was just a hair over $28,000. I'm printing these numbers because they lend credibility to what I'm about to say. But they aren't the main event. The main event is the simple fact that Paul started his bakery with almost no measurable business aptitude or training of any kind; that he is running it as a single guy without a partner; that he works 30–35 hours a week; that his crew consists of ordinary people, not superheroes; that his bread is among the best in the system; that he has no interest in books yet produces great income statements himself in four hours a month; that he always takes Sunday, Monday, and Thursday completely off; in short, that he is managing the fastest growth we've ever seen in a relaxed and unhurried way, with a sense of humor, seeming always to have all the time in the world for anything he wants to do. I returned from a visit to Salt Lake recently. I gave Paul some good ideas, felt like I earned my pay. But his bakery scored high points on every one of our important measures of quality.

And as I flew away from Salt Lake, I realized that I had spent the whole visit as student, with Paul as teacher. Laura and I came darn close to turning Paul down when he wanted a franchise. He didn't fit what we were looking for at the time. This is important to my story, so I'd like to include a little history here. Our first impression of Paul was that we really *liked him,* that he thought the same of us, that he was "pure Great Harvest"—excited about bread quality, generosity, not hung up on money. One of the things that was most striking to us was the complete lack of "pushiness" on Paul's part when it looked for awhile as though we would be unwilling to take him. The bakery was something he wanted very much, and he called us often just to talk and make sure that we hadn't forgotten him. But at the same time there seemed to be a complete acceptance that whatever we eventually decided, he would go with that decision and no hard feelings. At the time, we didn't really understand that this personality trait of quiet acceptance was something that we would come to rate very highly in looking at new people, something which would later prove to correlate solidly with the eventual success of the bakery.

But you can take a good thing too far. Paul was in his late thirties, with absolutely no savings to speak of, doing social work for $12,000 a year, no quantifiable business experience whatsoever. We agreed to take him only after getting his parents on the phone, explaining to them in vivid detail the risk they were undertaking in backing him, and making sure that they had a real clear picture of what a gory bakery failure was like. They needed to know there was a real chance they would lose all of the money invested in the bakery. After that, we went ahead with a clear conscience, knowing that we would give Paul a shot at it, but that there were some strong weaknesses that he would have to be aware of, and compensate for, if he were going to succeed. I still remember, on the location trip, trying purposely to steer Paul toward locations with low rent and low gross sales, something that would be easy for a single guy with no management ability to handle.

But everything about working with Paul was a delight. You might remember my story of the training—no cash register, nothing ready, just the bare minimum necessary to make bread, but a loose fun spirit that was pure Great Harvest. One of the most interesting things about Salt Lake was that, unlike Minneapolis, sales were nothing really special at first. In fact, for the first year, there was just the slow steady growth you see in any healthy bakery. Then, when the bakery was about a year old, it started growing in a subtle but definite exponential curve. We sit in our office and watch gross sales come in for new bakeries, and the numbers translate in our imagination to a view of what it must be like for the new people down at the bakery. Knowing Paul, and watching those gross sales, we *knew* we had a wreck on our hands. He just didn't have the manpower or the tools to deal with that kind of growth. And yet, when we'd call, Paul would be joking around, with plenty of time to talk.

Not only that, but we began to learn from experience that if we wanted to try something *new* in a bakery, Paul was one of the people in the system who had enough time and enough extra energy to play around and experiment. It's no coincidence that he was the first to go out and buy a 140-quart mixer, and figure out the plastic bowl extenders, and institute the new bowl system that everybody is switching to now. I'd like now to part with the simple facts, and give you two interpretations of what is going on in Salt Lake—Paul's, and my own. Each, I believe, is equally valid, the same animal seen from two different sides. I'm hoping that Paul will forgive me for printing this. I feel that, for anyone ready to receive these new ideas, what he told me is too important to have censored, even by Paul. Paul believes that this material shouldn't be talked about openly except to a willing student. I've already said that I go to him as student. I'm trusting that you will too.

Paul's Explanation

A little over three years ago Paul began a disciplined program of regular meditation and yoga. As you know from the last newsletter, Laura
and I have been meditating for over a year now, and we have always
had our regular outdoor runs, which have some of the same quieting
effects that yoga does. So although we are just learning, we're open to
Paul's ideas to begin with. A lot of the things that Paul says make sense
to us, because we've seen them ourselves, whereas they probably
wouldn't have a couple years ago. Anyway, Paul's regular routine is
45 minutes of meditation and 45 minutes of yoga. He also does something pretty physical like cross-country skiing, every weekend. He sees
this routine as a way of working on himself every day to get quiet
inside, a way for him to practice and perfect a different way of looking
at the world. He had been working in this way for about a year and a
half when he walked into the Boulder bakery and got the idea to do a
Great Harvest in Salt Lake. Paul describes the process of starting the
bakery as a meditative exercise. He specifically did not set any goals
or deadlines, but instead used the startup process as a form of practice
for becoming the work, as opposed to doing the work. He worked
super hard, and that was part of the process, but at the same time he
wasn't *pushing*. Paul says he has spent his whole life in psychology,
but that what he is doing now is exactly the opposite of all of his
training. The changes he has seen in himself have been gradual, almost
going unnoticed—from a frantic, success and goal-oriented feeling to
a detachment from events and a remarkable perspective. During his
45-minute meditations, it sometimes takes him over half an hour to
get past all the "drivel" as he calls it—new ideas for the business, what
he's going to eat for supper, a problem with the car, things like that.
He says if he skips a day, it takes him several days to build it back up
again. The process is impossible to teach. It's something that you just
have to do for yourself.

Many of Paul's management styles are exactly the opposite of regularly accepted business practice. I've known all my life, for example, that the way to get things done is to set clear goals and go for them as directly as possible. Paul says that you don't get anything of value until you don't want it, until you've broken your attachment to specific results. The exact dynamics of why this works you'll never know and it doesn't matter. He sees his role in managing the bakery as one of: 1) Going home, working on himself, getting quiet and clear; 2) Walking into the bakery and being fully accepting of anything that happens that day, using the bakery as practice for not getting "caught" by events; 3) Using the bakery as a practice ground for "getting out of the way" of the other people working there—being there for them, but not imposing his own desires or imposing models of how the day should turn out. He's still working hard, but his management is more by example than by design. He doesn't work so much according to a list as by walking in, seeing the bakery as an organism, and feeling what it needs, that particular day, to make it more healthy.

Paul's spiritual work at home gives him habits of working always in the present moment. He looks for what he can be doing *right now* that will most benefit the health of the bakery and the health of the people working there. He works at not having an opinion, pro or con, on the value of what he did yesterday. He works at forgetting any rigid models of what tomorrow will be like. Paul works hard at not judging his people, at accepting them unconditionally, just as they are. He believes he can do more good by working on himself than by trying to change other people. This kind of thinking gets pretty darn tricky when you're somebody's boss, as you might well imagine. For a long time Laura and I thought he was nuts. But paradoxically, Paul is a very effective boss. He teaches, instead of judging. He forgives mistakes. I believe that he loves his people way more than he loves his business. He cares more about those people, as people, than about perfection. Paradox or not, this is really at the root of being a great boss. In an atmosphere like this, people try new things, make mistakes, learn much quicker, and actually care about their work much more.

Before Paul started the bakery he had built for himself a strong faith that these techniques were powerful and useful. But they were still relatively untested in any sort of heavy duty working environment. The bakery was consciously planned as an experiment in meditative practice. He used the startup specifically as a meditation, taking it one day at a time, and never letting go of his 45-minute routines. The bakery was secondary to his daily practice, a daily challenge where he could use and perfect the techniques. He remembers getting caught every day in the chaos of the startup, losing touch with his training, then going home and working on himself some more. Each day was a routine of go to work, try to keep a quiet center, try to become the work, try to stay in the present moment, and when you lose it, go home and work on yourself some more. He has thirty or forty stories of times when this worked to his advantage in almost magical ways. One time, in one of the worst crises of the startup, he had an engineering problem which he couldn't solve—a support for the roof had to be removed, but the roof would then cave in. Paul's reaction was to go skiing. He was out there skiing, working on being unattached to the bakery, when he saw a guy zooming toward him on skis down the mountain, out of control. This guy fell right at Paul's feet, stood up, brushed off the snow, and they started talking. Turns out he was a carpenter, and he ended up solving the problem and helping Paul for the duration of the startup in return for free bread once the bakery got open. Paul doesn't try to explain phenomena like these, he just accepts them along with everything else.

The important point is that his reaction to chaos is to go home and work on himself first, then return and watch the chaos magically go away. The more successful Paul's bakery becomes, the greater it works for him as a vehicle for practicing non-attachment to goals or outcomes. Paul actually sees it that way, on a daily basis. He cares about the bakery, in the sense that he wants it to have maximum health. He cares that his actions are in line with the flow of things, everyday. But at the same time he works at having no preferences for outcomes or results. If you've done enough of this kind of inner work a "bad day" is just as perfect, just as correct and in the order of things, as a "good day." If a day comes when the bakery burns down or just no longer feels right, Paul hopes that he will be completely content with leaving it behind and going on to whatever is next for him in the order of things.

Pete's Explanation

There's a lot going on here. Most of you have learned to trust Laura and me for *solutions that work*, in real day-to-day bakery situations. I am as sure as I've ever been of anything that the phenomenal success of the Salt Lake bakery was engineered by a man who knew exactly what he was doing. It didn't happen by accident, it's not an anomaly, and it's something that we can all put to immediate use in our own businesses. Let me come at it from several different angles.

Angle #1: The VALS Typology

The answer that we're looking for is not as simple as, "The more you go home and meditate, the more money you make." It's not like Paul levitated himself to success sitting on a cushion. If it were that simple, all Laura and I would have to do to have a great franchise would be to recruit all our new people from yoga retreats. There's more to Paul Maurer than meditation and yoga. For one thing, his family. Paul's dad is retired now, but in his day he was one of the most successful building contractors in Salt Lake, and was in charge of overseeing LDS construction projects all over the world, as well as being a pillar of the Temple, which is *the* church in the Mormon faith. In other words, he was successful, an achiever of goals, a man able to decide what he wanted and get it. One of Paul's brothers is a psychiatrist in Seattle, and the other is a specialist M.D. in Salt Lake—they each make a lot of money and are very smart. The odds favored Paul being successful. But instead of going for money, he was attracted to psychology and social service and spent many years seemingly in the actual avoidance of money, following his own path.

Marvin Grulli introduced Laura and me to one of the most interesting books we've read in past years: *The Nine American Lifestyles*, by Arnold Mitchell. This is a long, detailed book, but basically it outlines something called the "VALS TYPOLOGY." I'm not going to go into this stuff much here. Suffice to say that this typology is the result of a lot of research done by some real smart people over a lot of years and spending a lot of money. VALS stands for "Values and Lifestyles Survey," and one of the things it's used for is in defining customer motivations in large market studies. There's a lot of money right now pouring into VALS research because it works so well at predicting outcomes in large marketing programs. Paul's dad and both of his brothers are probably pure Achievers under the VALS typology. Achievers are some of the happiest and most successful people in the United States, and comprise twenty percent of the population.

Paul broke away from the Mormon church and went off to become a deep-sea diver. This put him perhaps briefly as an I-Am-Me, then solidly in the Experiential category. After that, as is the way with many Experientials, he started gravitating toward helping professions and became pure Societally Conscious. At the time he made the decision to start a Great Harvest bakery, it's my belief that he was beginning to see some of the limitations of the Societally Conscious lifestyle. Along with a decision to return from Boulder to his hometown of Salt Lake was also a decision to return to a close relationship with his parents and, parallel with that, a resurgence of interest in the power of the Achiever's lifestyle. A very small percentage of the American population are what are called Integrated. Achievers and Societally Conscious are equally successful in money terms—between the two of them, they comprise most of successful people in this country. But there are some who reach the top of the Achiever ladder and see that there is more, that there is another side. Likewise, some reach the top of the Societally Conscious ladder, and see that the Achievers know some things that they've been missing. Paul Maurer, at this point in his life, meditating like crazy and making money faster than he cannot want it, surely classifies as an Integrated in the VALS typology.

This is why you can't just go to a yoga retreat and find successful Great Harvest owners. It's also why Laura and I can't just look for success in the corporate world and translate it straight across to a bakery. There's something very special about Great Harvest which requires Integrated owners for the optimum growth of the bakery. You have to love business, and also love quality and care about the health and well being of everyone and everything around you. One of the hallmarks of Integrated people is extreme effectiveness. They make things happen, things happen all around them, seemingly beyond any personal input of energy. Laura and I think of the Achiever side as the side where you listen to success tapes through headphones on the freeway, get programmed for Getting Things Done, then hit the deck and Make Things Happen. There's power on that side. We think of the Societally Conscious side as meditation, inner work, compassion, love; a strong and transparent vision of how everything fits together. There's every bit as much power on that side too. Integrated people are able to pull from both sources of strength. As rare as Integrated people are in the United States, I believe that a large percentage of Great Harvest owners fall into this category. It's probably more common to come at it from the Achiever's side—people who climbed quickly in corporations, saw the limitations of that life, and began to realize that there was something on the quality, Societally Conscious, small-is-beautiful side which they were missing. Like Paul, they too use their bakeries as a method for working on themselves. Paul used the bakery as a practice ground to strengthen his meditative training. Owners who come from the Achiever side use the bakery to break the grip of goal orientation and list making and find their way back to quality and concern for people.

Angle #2: Every Business Is
a Model of Its Owner

"Every business is a model of its owner." The more we travel to bakeries, the more we see that this is a truth to which there are no exceptions. Sometimes the results are funny, like the proverbial dog that looks just like its master. Sometimes they're sad.

Sometimes, the results are nothing short of miraculous. Everyone who has a business becomes a student of other businesses. You already know that all businesses are models of their owners. Think of all the times you've walked into a place, had great service, and known just what the owner of the place was like before you even met him. If you accept this rule as gospel, all sorts of corollaries fall into place. It's completely impossible to have a great business by giving yourself one hundred percent to the business and paying no attention to your personal side. On the other hand, it's entirely possible to do as Paul does, work on your personal side as a main event, and just have the business tag along wonderfully successful of its own free will.

There's a magnetism to the Salt Lake bakery that's hard to put your finger on. On one level, morale of the crew is excellent, mainly because Paul leaves them alone and they know they're good at what they do. There's pride in the bread, pride in cleanliness, all the usual things. But Paul talks of customers who come in and talk of feeling more than that—a sort of aura or magnetism to the bakery itself that can't quite be put into words. In Paul's bakery, that's just the business modeling its owner. The feeling is quieting, slightly humorous, vaguely spiritual.

There was a magnetism to our bakery in Great Falls too. But it was entirely different from Paul's. Laura and I were in our early twenties, and would routinely close the bars down dancing and getting drunk with friends, then go out to the 24-hour places for breakfast, then go in, still drunk, to make bread at 4 A.M. No one was allowed to play anything except hard rock and roll, and kneading time was everybody's favorite time, except of course for break. Break was so much fun that many times we'd have more people there who didn't work at the bakery than who did—boyfriends and other friends who just came to sit in on Great Harvest break. Kneading time was wall-to-wall laughing and joking, and we all wore shorts, even Kurt with his hairy legs. Morale was just as high as in the Salt Lake bakery, but for different reasons. In Salt Lake, the business reflects the owner's concern for people and quiet spiritual acceptance. In Great Falls, it reflected two people who were in it for a good time, in love, and out to have as much fun as possible with each day. We were *healthy* people in our twenties, Paul is a *healthy* person in his late thirties.

The point is that meditation doesn't have to be the method. It is one of the best. But the core concept is that YOUR BUSINESS WILL ALWAYS MODEL YOUR OWN PHYSICAL AND EMO-TIONAL HEALTH ALMOST EXACTLY. If you're bummed, your employees will be bummed, your customers will be bummed, and your income statement will be bummed. The key word is *health*. The key idea is that the health of the business *follows* from the health of the owners. There is no way your business will be as successful as it can be until you make your *first* priority your own physical and emotional health.

Angle #3: Handrails

There's a great word used in the sport of orienteering. Orienteering is using map and compass competitively. Competitors orienteer through forests and over mountains to checkpoints, and whoever can do it fastest without getting lost wins. A "handrail" in orienteering is any land feature which you can follow for a long time to keep from getting lost. For example, you might cut to the top of a ridge, then use the ridgeline for five miles as a handrail—when the ridge ends at a lake, you know exactly where you are. Creeks, valleys, ridges, all make good handrails in orienteering.

Don Stephenson made a very important point regarding Great Harvest startups. Don, as many of you know, had one of the highest status, highest skilled jobs in the United States Air Force, that of fighter-pilot trainer. He said that as much stress and quick reflexes as the job required, he was never put in a position quite like starting the bakery. The Air Force (or any other large organization) has a regular procedure for moving you ahead at your maximum rate of learning, but no faster. In a corporation, you get a promotion because you've learned your old job well. Your new job is a challenge, but it builds off the old and is something you can handle. People reach dazzling skill levels, like handling a fighter plane with a feather touch at full speed, by learning one little thing at a time in a series of manageable steps. As the sole owner of small business, though, there is no way to prepare in little steps for opening day. If the customers pour in, you suddenly need to be highly skilled as baker, boss, bookkeeper, the whole shot. A screwup in one department cascades into other departments and throws you off balance, and the customers keep pouring in. And there's no one just above you on the corporate ladder to say, "Whoa, I guess we fed it to you a little too fast there kid, let's back off and pace this thing a little slower." So you have chaos, too much too fast. And combined with that, an Operating Manual and a bunch of good teachers who have drilled into you that Quality is Critical, and Every Customer Gets the Red Carpet, and Take Time to Teach Your People, and the Place Should Be Spotless, and if you don't have Good Income Statements, You Die. This is what we students of Stress Management call "Values Bind." It can rip you apart, if you don't recognize what's going on.

You have a mind that is capable of constructing a thousand models of perfection, but WHAT IS is something different. Models are only handy tools. It takes a great deal of emotional wisdom, and, yes, emotional training, to be quiet and content with what actually *is*. And that inner quietness in the face of apparent chaos is the only way to see clearly, and make the best choices. Paul Maurer has a wonderful philosophy of living in the present, being content with what is, which stabilizes him when chaos hits. But all that philosophy misses the main point: YOU CAN'T JUST THINK LIKE THAT BY TRYING. YOU HAVE TO HAVE THE DAILY DISCIPLINES, METHODS—HANDRAILS—SOME WAY THAT YOU CAN *PRACTICE*, AND GET GOOD. I can think of a lot of people in the system who have great handrails, and some who don't. A handrail has to be something that you do everyday, and that you believe is so important that you would never give it up, not even if it meant the failure of your business. If Laura and I had to give up running or give up the franchise, we'd let the franchise go. Paul is the same way with his yoga and meditation. Mary Sparks told me she loved the bakery, but there was no way she would ever give up her power aerobics classes, no matter how badly they conflicted. Some people always make time for their kids, no matter what's coming down at work. Laura and I, in all the years we've been in business, never went without a two-day weekend, unless it was for the final burn going into a vacation. There were plenty of times, leaving for home, when we thought just one more day of effort might get us out of some awful jam. We just went home anyway. That's our handrail. In each of these cases, we held to our daily discipline, our old habits, with an almost religious tenacity, no matter what was happening to the business.

This is the essential requirement of a handrail. It's that magical point at which you say "My health and my happiness are number one. I won't set them aside, not even for a day, for the sake of the business." There's an analogy with all of this and resistance weight training. You start with light weights, and as soon as they get easy, you add more if you want to get strong. Paul learned meditation while living in a fairly quiet, stable routine. As his strength increased, he felt the need for more resistance—the chaos of a startup, the challenge of a thriving business. He added weight, and his strength grew. In Paul's case, he added weight very fast, but he gained strength very fast and he didn't get hurt. He kept hold of his handrail no matter what. There are plenty of other cases where the resistance increased too fast, broke people's grip on their handrails, and an awful period of two or three years followed in which they had to learn everything the hard way, or not at all.

I'm going to go public now, with Laura's permission, and list for you our personal handrails. I think it will be a surprise. I think that very few people realize how much time it really takes to keep yourself personally strong, to take proper care of your personal health when running a business. I believe very strongly that for a person in their thirties you need a *minimum* of one and a half hours per day of some sort of disciplined routine, and a two day weekend completely away from business. Paul meditates forty-five minutes and does yoga for forty-five minutes. Laura and I run or lift weights for an hour, and meditate for a half hour, minimum. I just can't lie to you and be one of these people who says a fifteen-minute walk three times a week is going to cut it. These are roughly in their order of importance to us:

A. *Exercise.* One hour per day minimum, one and a half hours if time. Run or bike two days, lift weights the third. Push your limits a little bit. Stretching (nonspiritual yoga?) every day.

B. *Diet.* Modified Pritikin—Pritikin with lots of wild meat and beer. No sugar, salt, fats. No empty calories. Especially no coffee. Important of course to physical health, but equally important for steady moods, low stress, seeing clearly.

C. *Meditation.* Many methods, many paths. Several good books recommended last newsletter. Paul has catalogues of great books and tapes if you want to get heavy. Thirty to forty-five minutes per day minimum.

D. *Sleep.* We need seven or eight hours, and we don't make many exceptions.

E. *Making Love.* Sorry, I won't tell you our rules. But we do have rules. There's discipline and regularity, it's not just

left up to chance. Some days we're too worn out for it to
come naturally, and the rules carry us along.

F. *Evenings, weekends, vacations.* We have a hard work–home
separation, a habit going back over fifteen years. We don't
talk about work at home or in the evening, we always take
a two-day weekend with the same can't-talk rule, we have
always taken a full month's vacation (recently increased to
six weeks). In the past couple of years, we've had to extend
the can't-talk rule to a can't-think rule. Can't-think is a
tough one. The meditation helps.

G. *Loves.* Marriage, kids, friends, family. Camping, hunting,
skiing, drinking, dancing. These things really don't belong
down on the list, they're actually the main event. It's just
that they don't classify quite as clearly as "disciplines."
Even so, though, discipline is important. We watch the
amount of time we are giving to our kids, we read stories
before bed, we go out on a date by ourselves once a month,
we go out with friends twice a month, we set aside a week
for hunting and a week for winter camping. Let me digress
for a quick point. If you work too hard too long, you un-
bond from your loves. Then something happens to convince you you're in trouble, and you remember the things
you used to love, and go back to them for strength. You
take four days off, and go skiing—but after only two days,
you realize you've outgrown skiing. It isn't actually all that
fun. It's cold, the lines are long. In fact, in a flash of inspiration, you realize what you really love now is your business, and you want to go back now, and fire John, and paint
the mixer . . . STOP. You are in bad trouble, my friend.
You might have to keep skiing a whole *week* to rebond.
Maybe you're so bad off you'll have to ski *all winter* to
rebond. That's your punishment for letting things get so
out of hand. There's only one way to be in love with life,

and that's to have loves. There's only one way to have loves, and that's to spend *time* with them. It doesn't matter if it's skiing, or kids. The bonding can't happen without the time. That's exactly why you overbond to business—you spend all your time there. If skiing used to be your favorite thing, it still is, down deep inside you. Take that on faith. Give it the time it needs to win your love back.

H. *Journal.* This is a new one for us, kind of different and kind of neat. Laura and I each spend ten minutes every morning right before work reading old entries or writing new ones in our journals. This is a sort of rational-side meditation, a chance just to play freely with new ideas, things we're excited about, in the privacy of pages no one else will ever read. Many times the entries take the form of fantasies or visualizations of a future we would like to see happen, or clear statements of goals. (Yes, we still write down goals. But of course we have no preferences about the outcomes!)

I. *Religion, Principles.* (Seems sort of bad putting principles last on the list. Oh well. It sure wasn't going to be making love or vacations.) We go to church once a month, religiously. We never lie, and we are big fans of the golden rule. These things are important handrails in their own right. Business is a great place to get lots of practice.

Angle #4: The Bottom Line

I've done my best to explain the phenomenon in Salt Lake, from several angles. I know that most of you agree, at least in principle, with much of what I've said. You might feel that I'm dramatizing or going overboard, but at the same time you recognize a kernel of truth. One very real question still remains to be answered: How, realistically, could all of this stuff possibly produce the phenomenon we are seeing in Salt Lake? How, realistically, can forty-five minutes of meditation possibly replace a couple working a combined one hundred hours a week of one hundred percent effort in a bakery? How can thirty-five hours a week of "getting out of the way" and a little personal-side hocus pocus beat out everybody else in the system in raw gross sales? What makes this stuff so effective? Laura and I both know the answer, we've seen it at work for years. It's something you just accept after awhile, after seeing it again and again and again. The first few times you really see it at work, you hardly believe your own eyes. Then after awhile, you just know it as a curious fact of nature. *The reason it works has to do with seeing clearly.*

When you pull away from the business, you give yourself slack, freedom of motion. You learn a different view of time. We all have the same twenty-four hours. Why do some people have all the time in the world, while others run around with a huge list that they'll never get done? It isn't that some people are born with more things to do. It's just two different ways of looking at the same world. These hand-rails, these disciplines, somehow create the all important slack in your life. After a vacation, Laura and I have known for years that we could count on seeing something brand new, in a brand new way, and making some great money-making change in our business. A business can't be run analytically, like some mechanic working on a car. There are lever points which are invisible from close up, invisible unless you have the distance and the slack to see clearly. Cutting a hot slice of bread for a customer, taking time to talk with an employee, having a few minutes for some phone calls to order a bigger mixer—these are the little things you never have time for, and yet they are where your effort is tremendously magnified.

Marvin Grulli was talking to me about the big restaurant he used to own. Those were tough times for him, living in the fast lane, short of time, too much to do. And yet he told me that, of all the things that pressed for his attention every day, he could see that there were two things he needed to be sure were done right—that he person-ally should be at the front door seating customers, and that the kitchen should be spotlessly clean. Why these particular two things, out of all the things you could be doing? Suppose two people are in a race to navigate their way across a giant complicated maze. The first person works at it a hundred hours a week, frantically racing down each blind alley, trying to overpower the thing by sheer physical exertion. The other person just works at it in his spare time, but can somehow see the maze from above, and never takes a wrong turn. Every one of his choices is the right choice at that moment. He wins.

We all find ourselves in two roles, the role of survivor, and the role of musician. Most of the things that we do, we do in survivor mode. We have strong instincts to get ahead, to get the dishes done, to accumulate stuff in case things go bad. But in the midst of all this getting ahead, we all find a little time for our music. For one person, the music is teaching his little girl to ski. For another, building a cedar strip canoe by hand. But in general, in America, we are overdeveloped survivors, underdeveloped musicians. A business can be music. By letting go of the survivor mentality—how near is starvation, really?—we can start to hear that music. We can teach it to the people who work for us. Our customers can hear it. And we learn that the music has power of its own. We can relax into it, and let it carry us and all the people around us. Great Harvest is full of this special music. We see it, hear it, smell it, taste it, everyday. It isn't Laura or me, or any one of you, or anything we do, individually. It's its own music, larger that the sum of all these little parts. We see it in the new people, caught up by the whole thing and wanting to be part of it. We see it in the old people, teaching and helping and forgetting to ask for pay. The more all of us in Great Harvest let go of our strong survivor reflexes, the louder and more moving music can become. Great Harvest, and each bakery in it, has enough music and power to grow on its own, if we all relax and just listen and get ourselves out of the way.

And this brings me to the bottom line. You can take all this power, and apply each of these techniques, and try to harness the energy of the music to build a stronger business, and it *won't work*. If you're doing it for the business, you still don't get it. It isn't until you really and truly do the business for yourself and your people that the forces align. Many years ago, Laura and I hiked the full width of the state of Montana, along the divide. Fall came, and we came down from the mountains, and decided to stay here. We looked for a good town where we could maybe make some bread, and ended up at the Davenport Motel, Great Falls, Montana, for a dollar a night. Just another good campsite along the trail. We made our bread so that we could save enough money to go hiking again, that next summer. With years and age and a successful business, it's easy to forget what a life is for. Reading books and newsletters on the best management thinking, it's easy to think you should have fun so you can be successful. But from our first day in business we have watched friends and acquaintances being sucked in by their work, and we've grown to have a healthy respect for the power of that whirlpool in the river. We have never let ourselves forget the feeling of coming down from the mountains, and making a little bread so we could go back.

15

A DIFFERENT
BOTTOM LINE

I called my friend Barry Vesser yesterday and asked him how to meditate. Barry lives on an organic farm and knows more about meditation than anyone I know, having spent a year at a Zen monastery in southern California. That and I switched to decaf coffee.

It's a start.

The changes that are coming over me since reading Pete's newsletter are small—a quicker smile here, more deep breathing when Valerie goes crazy on the little drum my mother gave her for Christmas, a little less need to get things done. It's good. The truth is I have a lot of work to do yet. I am one of those Achievers "who reach the top of the Achiever ladder and see that there is more, that there is another side," but who knows that reaching over to the other side will be work.

I decided to start my recommitment to Great Harvest by remembering why others are so devoted to it. Sure they love to bake excellent bread and make a good living, but is there something more, something deeper?

Bringing Love to What They Do

I've always said the best owners in Great Harvest are religious, in the broadest sense of the word, that they bring *love* to what they do. Now I also see they are Integrators. They stand half in one world and half in another, one foot in the world of getting-things-done and another in the world of seeing-things-as-they-are.

You see it in Bonnie Johnson Alton, the store owner from St. Paul, Minnesota. She gets things done. Her bakery records are neat and in order, her income statement percentages in line with system norms. Her bread is locked down—she rarely bakes a loaf that is anything but delicious, and her promotion is steady and effective. I'd hate to see the to-do list she carries around in her head; I know it's a monster, but she works through it with the ease of a well-trained athlete.

For all her efficiency, though, there is another side of her. I asked her how she saw her business, and she didn't talk about how much money it put to the bottom line or next year's projected growth. She said, "The work I do is really a form of ministry. The generosity we have in the store is unconditional and reflects the unconditional grace that is a part of my faith."

I am not sure why Great Harvest seems so suffused with this integrating sensibility, but I have a sneaking suspicion it is because of the bread. On the one hand, the fact that it takes money to start a bread store guarantees our ranks will be filled with Achievers. It is mostly Achievers who at relatively young ages amass the cash necessary to build a bakery. They've figured out some way to make money, and it shows up on their balance sheet. The bread seems to draw another type as well. There is something ancient about fresh-baked whole-wheat bread, something that recalls a simpler, more wholesome time. That something is like a magnet to people who want more from life than a Lexus and vacations in St. Thomas.

It's the Bread

"Making bread is honorable," says Tom Cordova. "There is something very grounding in that. To me it's like digging in the dirt or gardening. I'm not really sure why, but it makes me feel better as a person."

The word "simple" is a clue. Our bread is simple. As I've noted already, our most basic breads are just whole-wheat flour, salt, water, yeast and something sweet. In fact, one of the tag lines that has found the most use in the system is "Bread—Keep It Simple!" Owners are proud to make an uncomplicated product and want to let customers know it is one of their core values. Simplicity is, it seems to me, a code word for this thing that Achievers crave. The world of Achievers is one of complexity: huge lists of things to get done, tightly managed time, a powerful and practiced ability to multitask—drive the kids to day care, slip the French tapes into the tape deck on the way, check your voicemail on the cell phone. Efficiency is the highest value. Keep moving, we tell ourselves. Keep working the list.

Then someone like Tom waltzes into our lives, telling us that "Bread is the Thing—Keep It Simple!" And it is like a cool balm for sore muscles. For many owners the fact that they own a bread store is a wonderful combination of achievement and something else, like it was for Paul Maurer.

If Great Harvest owners were just Achievers, they wouldn't understand the simplicity that's right at the heart of what they sell. Likewise, if they were just Societally Conscious recruits from the nearest seminary, the business would fall in on itself for lack of attention to the things that make businesses strong. In the bread business, you need both—love *and* strength.

Something Bigger

Bonnie Johnson Alton tells the story of a young man who started working as a kneader in her bakery on a Friday. He spent that first day
getting down the basics, trying to master the mechanics of shaping the
bread to Bonnie's satisfaction. Saturday morning he was in again, able
now to take his eyes off of what his hands were doing for a second or
two to survey what was happening around him. Around 10:00 A.M.
he saw it: St. Paulites flooding into Bonnie's parking lot and walking
toward the bakery. The young man was amazed. "You mean people
get up on Saturday morning and say to themselves, 'I want to go to
Great Harvest'?"

"Yes," said Bonnie, "they do."

It's Bonnie's neighborhood bread store—get your weekly dose of
the simple life here. Fill yourself up. Get recharged.

Religion is not just figuring out the right balance between being an
Achiever and being Societally Conscious. It is about being connected
to something transcendent that gives our lives meaning. When I say
many Great Harvest owners seem religious to me, it is because of the
thought they give to the larger context in which they have chosen to
live their lives.

One of the things I love best about working for Great Harvest is
how so many people seem to mine meaning from it in different ways.
Here are four "causes" I hear people within Great Harvest describe,
four ways in which what we do is meaningful to them.

- "We are building a whole-wheat nation." This is the idea that
  we are about: hot, healthy whole-wheat bread for everyone,
  everywhere, all the time. We are proud that we make bread,
  not nuclear weapons. Simple nourishing good food, in a
  country where real food is getting hard to find. We are,
  through our bread, a force for good. We bake a bread that is
  as honest and nutritious as any food on the planet.

- "We help people lead free, happy lives." You hear this one a lot from owners, particularly in reference to their employees. Paula King, owner of the store in Lexington, Kentucky, says, "In this business you touch so many lives and don't even know it. I just got a letter from a former employee saying that Ron and I had taught her important things about work and life. To me that makes it all worth it." You hear this also at the franchise office. Says Pete Wakeman, "My top cause is more the franchise itself, the freedom in it, people living fully, truly entrepreneurial lives, free to play in their businesses, yet connected together for the excitement of quick learning. My cause could be called 'free-networked self-employment.' "

- "We are creating a more perfect world." Bob Garrett, who owns the bakery in Lawrence, Kansas, is famous in Great Harvest for his "little world" speech at a session some years back when we were coming up with our mission statement. Here is a description of that talk, taken from a newsletter article written by Pete Wakeman about the meeting. "Bob takes all new people aside when they first hire on in Boulder. . . . Bob used to manage the Boulder, Colorado, store, before opening his own in Kansas . . . and sits them down, and tells them what this business is about. He says Great Harvest is the best chance you may ever get to create a little world that's exactly how you wish the world could be. You can make it as fun as you like. You can make it so everyone cares about each other and supports each other. You can do quality, without having to compromise. Whatever you care most about, you can make a little world out of just this bakery, these co-workers, these customers. That little world can be exactly the way you want the big world to be. And that little world can make the big world better."

- "We are creating community." Tom Amundson says, "People come up to us all the time and tell us how grateful they are for the sense of community we bring to this area. We are a meeting place. They tell us we have created something special. Frankly, I am not sure how we've done it, but I do know I am proud of it and it is meaningful to me." Debbie from the franchise office adds, "Most of all, the thing I love about Great Harvest is the people. I love the people in the franchise office and I love the owners of our stores. I love being part of a group of smart, caring people."

Lots of businesses suffer because they ignore the powerful need people—owners, employees and customers—have to feel as if they are part of something larger than themselves in order to feel as if they are participating in something good or some sort of cause.

All the causes owners talk about work together to create a job that feels meaningful to me. I'd probably add one more cause to the list:

- "We are all part of a grand experiment." Great Harvest is reinventing the way people work together. Lots of our franchise friends tell us we are crazy to try and build a freedom franchise, but we're having a blast trying anyway. I love the fact that people in our system have complete freedom to create their lives the way they want, but to do so within a caring, supportive community. This could be the seed from which a powerful new business model might grow.

I think most people are like me. I need to feel that my life is part of something bigger. Indeed, it is part of something larger, it is just that sometimes I need help seeing it.

. . .

When I was a Peace Corps volunteer in the small Cameroonian town of Njinikom, I had a best friend named Peter Akuo. He lived with his family in a small compound at the bottom of a steep hill, down in the valley where the women of the village farmed. Near the trail that went out to the fields, Peter had a small roadhouse. The mud floor of the hut kept it cool and the place was stocked with orange soda and bottles of Beaufort beer. Most evenings, he and I would go up to the roadhouse, drink a bottle or two, and listen to Makossa on his battery-powered record player. My usual place was on a bench along the east wall. There, pinned into the mud brick was an old moth-eaten map of the continent. Missing most of North Africa and everything south of Angola, that worn picture of Africa seeped into my subconscious over the course of two years. We'd laugh and gossip in the pidgin common to that part of Cameroon. Then after an hour or so, the conversation would turn local and everyone would revert to Itiakom. I'd struggle to follow along, but about halfway through the second beer, my mind would wander and slowly focus on this huge map of the African equator.

When I finished my service in the Peace Corps, I got it into my head to walk across Africa, west to east along the equator. Lots of people since then have asked me why, and it was simply because of that map. After staring at it for two years, I had to go see all those places whose names I had memorized—Sangmalima, Yoko-douma, Bangui, Dar Es Salaam.

The odds against my making it all the way across the continent were great. Not only was it a physical and mental feat to walk that far, but also there was good chance that local officials would keep me from my goal or that sickness would trip me up.

On September 15, 1986, though, I vowed to give it a shot. I woke up early, took a swim in the Atlantic just north of Kribi in southwestern Cameroon, slung my big blue pack on my back, and started walking east.

The trip was great fun, but it was a constant battle to maintain my mental focus and keep on walking. It was hot. My feet hurt. But I had a goal and so I kept the pressure on. That goal—to walk across Africa—stood over me like a drill sergeant, yelling in my ear whenever

I started to lag—"GET going! One foot in front of other. Move! Move! Move! Don't stop until you taste the Indian Ocean." And it worked. I knew what I wanted, and I was bound to achieve it.

There was another voice as well, that told me to mellow out, enjoy the trip. Like a pixie flitting around my head, it would whisper, "This is great! Look at those butterflies. Can you believe you are hacking your way through a dense forest with a machete in your hand? If for some reason you don't make it across, you'll have had quite an adventure so don't sweat the goal too much. Your job is to be here, now. Work on being present to the beauty. Life is not some means to an end."

I often look back on that trek and ask myself what I learned. As things turned out, I did not make it all the way across the continent. A bad case of hepatitis stopped me in what was then Zaire. But I did walk more than a thousand miles, and I did have a world-class adventure, but what did it all mean? Did I fail? Did I succeed?

I think I learned this: there are two gods in our lives—the god of progress and the god of peace. There are two forces, they pull us in different directions—one toward achievement and the other toward acceptance. Our job is to know these two gods and to hold lightly in our hands the truth they embody. I've always liked the way F. Scott Fitzgerald put it in *The Crack-Up*, "The test of a first-rate intelligence is the ability to hold two opposed ideas in the mind at the same time, and still retain the ability to function." Life requires this of us: to know, respect, and use the power of getting things done, but also to know, respect, and use the power of seeing things as they are. The trick in life is to integrate the two.

It isn't easy. The Ayn Rand in us wants to remake the world in our image, but the Pooh wants to laugh and recount our honey pots because, "that's what I like to do." Both forces are powerful. Look to the West's triumph in the world, and you see a culture that has successfully made a religion of progress and getting things done. Much that we see around us—the steady availability of food, shelter so ubiquitous that it ceases to concern most of us, technology that races to remake our lives and the nature of community—all this is the direct result of human beings pushing themselves to do the seemingly impossible. Progress is clearly a force for good in our world.

But progress has its mirror in peace, a force that urges us to be satisfied and to count our blessings. A force that urges us to see ourselves as a strand in a larger fabric and to relinquish the profound sense of self that keeps us from realizing we are all one—bits of cosmic dust bound together in our commonness. This force, too, is alive in our world. It's what keeps monasteries open and busy, it writes the holy texts; and it is the wellspring from which most wisdom seems to flow.

But how to integrate the two? Is it a balancing act? Run around all day chasing goals and sit in meditation at night? Or is there a better way? Wondering if maybe Pete Wakeman has already written on this, I dug through more old files and I found this gem:

> I was doing my journal this morning like any other morning, and for fun I went reading around in my old stuff. I rediscovered a little how-to. I like it. It puts me in a good mood.
>
> You'll notice it has two equal parts, labeled focus, and freedom. It's my belief that your brain acts as what cognitive scientists call a "difference engine." A difference engine is nothing more than a 4-part system, with one part that creates an exact picture of a goal, another part that creates an exact picture of reality, a part that compares goals with reality, and a part that acts physically on the world to move the two together. Simple little goal-seeking robots are built this way; so are insects. Sounds weird, but why it's important is that it explains a lot about human happiness, or unhappiness. Strong goals, and pictures of what could be, are good. Seeing the world clearly, perfectly, just the way it is, is also good. "Truth waits for eyes unclouded by longing." But just as true: "All great achievement is fueled by burning desire."

I call the goal-setting, thinking side Focus, and I call the clear-seeing side Freedom.

It's highly unskillful to use your brain to mix these things. Mixing them causes unhappiness; they exist to serve you well, but only when apart. Skillful thinking keeps both sides very separate, views both with respect, and compares the two—the beautiful but fictitious goal, with the beautiful and very real world—in a peaceful way, to choose a precise course of action.

This model sounds right to me. What Pete calls focus, I call progress. What he calls freedom, I call peace. But we are talking about the same thing. Our job is to see each of these forces for what they are—part of the normal and healthy functioning of our heads, both playing a real role in how happy we are.

Since reading Newsletter #46, I am trying to spend a little more time "working on myself." I am running, but I am also spending about a half an hour a day doing yoga and every other day lifting weights. These latter two are new for me. The yoga teaches me how to relax into "progress." "Don't push," yoga-types are fond of saying; "just breathe, and you'll get better with time." No goals, just sit in the positions and breathe; the rest will follow. The yoga is good for me. It helps me deepen my peaceful side. The weights give me a good outlet for my natural goal-setting side. I'm learning that you don't make any progress with weights unless you set yourself goals and push what you think you can naturally do. Both are fun—one emphasizes flexibility, the other strength.

I was writing yesterday and decided to take a break and go for a short run. As soon as I left the house, my mind started reeling with all sorts of good stuff I should add to this chapter. I kicked myself for not bringing my little digital recorder to get some of the thoughts out. Then I laughed. I remember telling Laura Wakeman that I had a little recorder and I liked taking it running to record my thoughts as they came tumbling out. She looked shocked. "How could you do that?"

she said almost plaintively. "How could you ruin a run like that?" I'm realizing that, for her, running is about entering the temple of peace. It stuns her that anyone would even consider profaning it with a tool so obviously borrowed from the world of progress.

This is a clue, I decide. One of the ways Laura and Pete keep the balls of peace and progress in the air is to compartmentalize clearly what they are doing. Digital recorders are about progress. Running is about seeing peace, and never shall the two meet. Suddenly all this emphasis on forty-hour workweeks and work–home separation makes more sense to me.

One of the scariest moments in my life was on my walk across Africa when I caught a bad case of malaria. I was two days' walk from a village when the hallucinations started. Malaria isn't quiet or subtle. It assaults you with the kind of viciousness you might normally associate with thugs from Queens. One minute you are fine, maybe a little weak and achy. The next you can't see straight, unsure of where you are and barely coherent.

I was in western Cameroon where the forest is thick and gorillas commonplace. After passing through a string of pygmy villages, I saw the trail grow thin and less sure of itself. I kept moving, sure I would pop out the other side if I just kept the faith. Which is when the malaria hit. I remember falling down under a bamboo stand, my blue pack with the machete sticking out the top tumbling to the side. My simple African-style tunic was soaked with perspiration. My hair was matted and wet. Then I didn't know where I was.

I think I slept for five or six hours because it was dark when I awoke. There as I lay alone listening to the noises of the forest, the chills came—a slow ripple of cool at first, then a violent arctic blast. I shook so hard my teeth rattled and my head ached. It was the longest night of my life.

And then came the hallucinations. I saw the forest hogs and their pygmy pursuers. I saw the vines drop from the trees and snake their way around my legs. I saw a pair of black mambas with eyes as red as hot blood. And I saw the forest panther—the ghost of the jungle.

When the hallucinations released me exhausted toward dawn, they left me with a glimmer of another side, of a big world that knows not you and me but only all of us together. Burned into a tight little corner of my brain by the malaria and high fever was a third eye—able, if I let my mind go enough, to see the quivering ribbons of heat and light that tie us all together.

This is something I now see as a missing link. A way not so much to reconcile my two gods—the god of quiet and the god of noise—but to see them in a different way, to see them as the offspring of a common parent, a life force in the universe.

16

THE SECRET RECIPE

As the malaria passed, I walked half a day on through the forest and came, after a time, to the smallest of villages. It was really just a hunter's camp with two makeshift huts—one for a young man and another for his elderly father. The hunter was gone, leaving the old man there alone to tend to his small, barely capable fire.

Pitching to the left, and then to the right, in my weakness, I stumbled into the clearing and sat down on a felled log by the fire with the old man. For a long time, I didn't say anything. Neither did he. Then, after poking the low embers for almost ten minutes, he got up slowly, hobbled to his hut, and returned with a green plastic pail full of cool, clear water and a small gourd with which to ladle it. I lifted my head and gave him a weak smile.

Nearly an hour passed. Then the old man spoke. Slowly, and in heavily accented French, he said, "Sir, I must ask you a question: Are you a ghost?" He asked the question deliberately but without fear. I was taken aback. This old man plainly thought I was some spirit from the forest.

"No, I am not a ghost!" I said. "I am a silly white man trying to walk across Africa who is very, very sick. But I am sure I must look like a ghost." Relief fell across his face. "Yes, you do!" he said, the wrinkles around his eyes and across his face erupting into a broad smile and then he gave a deep laugh.

For the next week, this old man—his named turned out to be François—nursed me back to health. Every day he would disappear for an hour or two, walking into the forest that surrounded the compound and returning with an assortment of strange-looking grasses and herbs. He'd drop them into a big kettle of boiling water, then have me inhale the steam, gently draping a towel over my head and the pot to make sure none of the healing vapors escaped.

I am convinced, however, it was not his concoctions that healed me; it was his good humor and ready laugh. Every morning he would wake me at 5:00, yelling, "Get up ghost-boy. Time to go haunt the old African!" The rest of the day he would alternately poke fun at and encourage me, telling me tall tales of his hunting prowess and ribbing me good-naturedly on the foolishness of my expedition.

I'll never forget the choice François made that first day. Into his life came something odd and even a little scary, and yet he chose to roll with it and keep on laughing. I am sure François is now dead, it's been fifteen years since I bid him good-bye, but I still feel him like a kind of angel—a light, healing soul who stays with me and reminds me to bring laughter to whatever I do. Unbeknownst to me, François's playful attitude prepared me for what I was to learn at Great Harvest years later.

The Ingredients

At Great Harvest we spend a lot of time talking about recipes. Who has the best recipe for Dakota bread? How much cinnamon should a baker put in a batch of raisin bread? I have begun to see, however, that in between all this talk of whole-wheat flour and gallon measures, we are working together on another, deeper formula, a set of

learnings that taken as a whole are a recipe for how to create meaningful work and a good life. Here is the not-so-well-known recipe I've
learned:

- *Happiness comes from making choices.* This means not leaving
  your options open but making commitments. Rand Kunz
  said it best when he compared work to a marriage and ob-
  served that if you keep "looking," it makes you miserable.

- *We must design our lives.* Most people lead lives designed by
  others—their boss, their spouse, the clerk at the utility company who says a late fee will be assessed for nonpayment.
  Very few live their lives on purpose. In Laura and Pete Wakeman I have found a couple who has risen to the challenge
  and met it with grace. They said they wanted to live in Montana, hike a lot, bake great whole-wheat bread, and help others find the freedom they found. The clarity of their vision
  created the life they wanted to live.

- *Being obsessed about everything in life is impossible, but being
  wildly enthusiastic about one thing is required.* I think about the
  two Petes—Pete Rysted and Pete Wakeman—talking about
  bread and, in particular, how Pete Wakeman said that any
  successful business—and I'd say life—has to be uncompro-
  mising in one area of quality. Passion, as Lisa Wagner—our
  franchise chooser—said, is one of the clearest manifestations
  of a happy and successful person.

- *We must align the work we do and the businesses we own with
  the purposes of our lives.* We get seduced into thinking we must
  work for the businesses and work communities we create,
  when, in fact, they should be incontrovertibly in service of
  our lives. Tom and Sally of Minneapolis own one of the biggest stores in the Great Harvest system, but it is not the sole

focus of their lives. Instead they use their business to create time for their kids and do things they love, like attending the Birkenbeiner, an annual cross-country ski race in upstate Wisconsin.

- *When we are free to be ourselves and then connect together in a caring community, strange and wonderful things result.* The lesson of the learning community is that we can successfully combine real autonomy with collaboration and that such communities have impressive abilities to create innovation and adapt rapidly.

- *Products made with simple, whole ingredients combined with skill and love nourish and rejuvenate.* I never stop being amazed at the role good whole-wheat bread plays in our lives and in the lives of our customers. Good, wholesome products give us the energy to be who we want to be.

- *Authenticity is something to be cherished.* When we give people the room to express their undiluted creative nature, they jump at the opportunity with their whole selves and the result is a richer, more interesting world.

- *If we want to create a healthy world, we need healthy organizations, and to create those, we must first work on ourselves.* Paul Maurer, former owner of the Salt Lake City bakeries, meditates daily and allows work to develop naturally out of this. Where there are problems, his first response is, "I must go home and work on myself."

- *Honest generosity is like sunshine in its power to brighten the lives of those around us, as well as our own.* When we give without expectation of return, we create an energy in ourselves, which makes us and our communities stronger.

These are the ingredients of a good life and of strong work.
Combine them together and excellent things happen. But are they
enough? Is this the secret recipe? Or is there more? I'm still not completely sure. I decide once again to go for a run and listen for an
answer.

Along the Ditch

In 1963, the Bureau of Land Reclamation dammed the confluence of
the Red Rock River and Horse Prairie Creek to form Clark Canyon
Reservoir south of town. The purpose of the dam was not to generate
power but to irrigate. By raising the level of the reservoir, the BLR
was able to bring water to many acres of dry land high above the valley
floor using a system of ditches. The main ditch, really a briskly flowing
stream, flows by Dillon, east of town. Along its side runs a small service road, nothing more than two tracks through the sagebrush, really.
It's a great place to run, getting you out of town and up into the
foothills that surround Dillon.

I lace on my New Balances, head up White Lane, and then take a
left on the ditch road, alone with my thoughts.

They turn to Pete Wakeman. One of his favorite things to say
regarding this business is, "It is only bread!" It is his way of reminding
us that business is not the sum of who we are, and that we shouldn't
take it too seriously.

Pete, I decide, is talking about attitude. Some days, work goes well.
Other times, things fall apart. Regardless, each of us has total freedom
to choose our attitude. We can laugh at our mistakes or allow them to
tie us into knots. We can be in love with life or let the bumps throw
us. I remember a newsletter article Pete wrote a few years back describing what for him would be the worst possible day imaginable in
a bakery and his remarkable conclusion, which still gives me pause
and makes me think.

The oven develops this crazy problem, where all the shelves catch on the door ledge as they go by, flipping full bun pans into the bottom. Then the mixer makes a bad noise, gives off a smell, and stops. All the doughs are made and it's a hot wheat, rising fast. Yesterday two people were burned out of commission in a flour dust explosion, so I'm a little short staffed. The fire marshal just popped in to say if she has any say-so (which she does) I'll never mill flour again. This is beginning to stress me out. So I call home for a shoulder to cry on. Unbeknownst to me, my marriage of twenty years just unraveled, and she's gone. With the kids.

It's probably time to call this a truly bad day, quit, and get a fresh start tomorrow. So I carry dough to the Dumpster in buckets. This pulls my back so badly I just have to lie there between the Dumpster and the cardboard boxes, staring up at the telephone wires, and wait. The afternoon guy (whom I was going to fire for his crappy attitude, until the flour explosion) finds me two hours later. He asks me (I'm still on my back, looking up at him) if I meant to leave all those bowls over-flowing with dough in the back room?

(By the way, this story is a cinch for me to write, since it's one of my recurring bakery nightmares. I have versions of this one about twice a year, and always wake up sweating and pant-ing like a scared dog.)

Is this serious? No, actually, if it were to happen just this way, it would just be life! If you get frightened by a day like this (and most people would), you'll turn serious. Nobody would blame you. But the seriousness isn't in the world, it's in your head. Nothing, nothing, nothing is serious. The minute you get serious about something, it means you're frightened, if only a little bit.

What was Pete saying? Sure, seriousness and fear can bind you up; you can get to thinking that something is more ultimate than it is.

But what else? I think he is recommending what Laura wrote many years ago when she penned the first line of the mission statement, "Be loose and have fun." When I first read this, I couldn't believe a company would set its course by such a "non-businesslike" bearing. Now years later, I've experienced its magic. Again and again, I've seen people in the Great Harvest system bring joy to their world. I think of the day Scott Creevy, in a fit of inspiration, spraypainted the mission statement on his bakery's wall, or Vic and Linda Hanick's tradition in Kansas City of dressing up on Halloween, or Tim Heeren of Wichita, Kansas, and his knack for reminding nearly everyone there is fun to be mined in any moment. Great Harvest has created a community that doesn't take itself too seriously, and the result is freeing.

Look at that sentence, "Be loose and have fun." What does it mean to you? To me, it means "roll with things," "hold life lightly in your hands," and "accept life for what it is." It is the opposite of "being tight," always struggling to make things the way you want them, which is what I think Pete Wakeman is talking about when he says that nothing in life is serious. Only people's thoughts are serious. "Being loose" implies a certain detachment from outcomes, because when we fight too tenaciously for what we want, it is almost always because we are scared of what is going to happen next. Tightness comes from and leads to fear. When fear asserts itself, love is chased into the corner, deprived of another opportunity to brighten. "Having fun" means noticing and taking joy in life. It is, as François showed me, the choice to laugh even when faced with scary monsters.

And so it comes to this: *"being loose and having fun" is the secret that makes the recipe work.*

A Sense of Wonder

This is all fine, but how exactly do we pull this off, and incorporate "being loose and having fun" into our lives? Even if this is how we want to be, life has a way of conspiring to make that difficult.

I trot up to the house, sweat pouring down the back of my neck. The sun is hot and I ran hard. I cool down on the back porch and then walk inside where Mary hands me our newborn son, Wilson.

As I look into his eyes, I ask myself if I could tell him one thing in this world, what would it be? I think it would be this: *in awe, the world is always new; and in wonder, we can live a life of love and joy.*

I remember the first time I pulled hot Great Harvest bread from the oven. I was in Naperville, Illinois, apprenticing myself to John and Michelle Jefferds in their bakery. It was around 10:00 in the morning and I was alone as a baker for the first time since joining Great Harvest.

I slipped on the padded oven mitt, flipped the rod that stops the racks from rotating, slid the oven pan out on the now flat oven door, poked and prodded the bread until I was satisfied it was ready to pull, and then eased the big-trays out of the oven. There for the first time was my bread cooling on the racks. I couldn't believe it. I had made something with my own hands, and it was good. I caught the eye of a woman in the store who spoke to Michelle at the front counter and saw her excitedly pointing to the loaves. She wanted one. I was proud and happy, awed at what I had created.

Remembering this sense of wonder, I realize that "seeing the moments" is at the heart of being able to step aside from fear, embrace love and life, and be loose and have fun.

When I think of all I've learned at Great Harvest, in the end, the most important advice I have been given is to appreciate this wonderful lightness of existence. In so doing, I have begun to gain a grip on the steep pitch of my own life. I've also learned that this wonder doesn't just happen. It requires constant attention and cultivation, day by day and hour by hour, but the reward is great—a well-lived life, good work, and an abiding sense of celebration.

AFTERWORD

In April 1999, Scott Biniak called from the advertising agency Weiden and Kennedy to ask if the firm could come visit Great Harvest in Dillon and talk about the possibility of featuring us in a commercial about Microsoft.

I agreed and he sent out a team to ask us questions about how we worked and how we used computers to link owners together. A month later he called to say the agency wanted to set up a filming date. The result was four ads—one featuring the Great Harvest office in Dillon and three others featuring owners around the system. It was quite a little boon. The ads aired for nine months and were backed up with a print campaign.

I was in several of the ads and was pleasantly surprised when I started receiving royalty checks from Weiden and Kennedy's talent agency. Seems it wasn't enough that Microsoft was touting our company for free, they had to pay union wages to everyone who appeared in the ads.

Mary and I make a point to do fun things with unexpected money, so we decided to buy a tipi with the cash. We called it the "Where Do You Want to Go Today?" tipi and set it up on a friend's ground on the banks of the Big Hole River. We get there most weekends with the kids and lounge about and swim in the river.

I'm there now, finishing up the book and feeling thankful: thankful for my family; thankful for the blue sky; and thankful for all the people who helped me write this book. I look up from my laptop at the big twenty-four-foot poles converging at the top of the tipi and say a little prayer.

I've started praying recently. It is a new thing for me. I'm not very plugged into organized religion and so am not all that sure what to do, but still I try. There are two kinds of prayers I like. The first is an appeal. "Show me the way," I say quietly. The other is a prayer of thanksgiving, "Thank you for my life, and thank you for Mary's love." There is much to be thankful for.

·   ·   ·

I'd like to thank a number of people who have helped me write this book. First, thank you to everyone in the Great Harvest system. This book is about how much I've learned at your knee. The owners who have spent time with me both in preparation for this book and for other reasons are many. I owe you all a huge debt. You helped create this book, but more importantly I am a different and better person for having spent time with you. There is no finer collection of people anywhere. Thanks in particular to Tom Amundson, Joyce Conners, Tom Cordova, Bonnie Johnson Alton, Paula King, JoEllen Kunz, Rand Kunz, Pete Rysted, Brian Turner, Sally Weissman, and Terri Wynn for letting me interview them.

And thank you to everyone in the Dillon office of Great Harvest. I count you all as my friends. Thanks for your support and your passion. It's inspiring.

Of course, thank you to Laura and Pete Wakeman for starting Great Harvest. It's the best bread in the world and one of the most interesting little companies around. Not bad for twenty-five years' work! Your leadership and vision make us stronger and better people.

Thanks for showing us the way, and thank you for encouraging me to tell the story.

Thanks to two authors on writing: Anne Lamott for her wonderful and funny little book, *Bird by Bird: Some Instructions on Writing and Life*, and Susan Shaughnessy for her inspirational *Walking on Alligators: A Book of Meditations for Writers*. I turned to you when I got bogged down and you always lifted me back up. Thank you also to Maggie Klee Lichtenberg for your expert advice and patient coaching throughout this process. You helped keep me on the straight and narrow.

Thanks to those outside of Great Harvest who let me interview them, in particular Phil and Laurie Ferda, Eileen Bennett, Ray Dessault, and Scott Johnson.

A big thank you to my team of readers—Barry Vesser, Jackie McMakin, Sherri Alms, Peter Gross, Mary McMakin, Dave McMakin, Pete Wakeman, Laura Wakeman, Debbie Harrison Huber, and Mike Basile. It takes guts to tell someone, whom you know and like, that they "seriously missed the boat in Chapter 3" or "forgot to mention why this was important in Chapter 7." I really appreciate the time and courage it took to tell me the truth.

Thanks to Dianne Pelletier for typing in Pete Wakeman's old newsletter articles early in the process and to Dawn Eisenzimer for helping me reconcile differently edited copies of the book toward the end.

Thanks to my agent, Sheree Bykofsky in New York—you stuck with me when it wasn't at all clear this was going to work out—and to my editor at St. Martin's, Kelley Ragland. You showed me the book was equal parts Great Harvest story, business how-to, and notes to myself, and encouraged me to give generous attention-to all three. Thanks also to Ben Sevier at St. Martin's for your good cheer and efficiency.

Thanks to my folks—Dave and Jackie. You taught me to work hard but not to take life too seriously. And you gave me all of your love. Who could ask for more? Thanks to my sister, Peg, for standing with me, uncritical and affectionate throughout.

And finally, a huge kiss and a bouquet of the world's prettiest irises for Mary, the love of my life. Without your strong support, friendship, and love, it just wouldn't have happened.

Dillon, Montana
July 4, 2000

GREAT HARVEST BREAD CO. LOCATIONS

For specific location information, visit
www.greatharvest.com.

ALASKA
Anchorage

ARIZONA
Tucson

CALIFORNIA
Chico
Laguna Niguel
Oakland
Santa Barbara

COLORADO
Arvada
Boulder
Colorado Springs (2)
Denver
Ft. Collins (2)
Littleton

CONNECTICUT
Manchester
West Hartford

IDAHO
Boise
Idaho Falls (2)

Pocatello
Twin Falls

ILLINOIS
Arlington Heights
Bloomington
Champaign/Urbana
Evanston
Geneva
LaGrange
Naperville
Northbrook
Oak Park
Rockford

INDIANA
Evansville
Indianapolis (4)
Lafayette
Mishawaka
South Bend
Munster

IOWA
Des Moines

KANSAS
Lawrence

Overland Park
Wichita (2)

KENTUCKY
Lexington (2)
Louisville (2)
Middletown
Owensboro

MARYLAND
Annapolis
Pikesville
Rockville

MASSACHUSETTS
Lexington
Newtonville

MICHIGAN
Ann Arbor
Birmingham
Brighton
Commerce TWP
Farmington
Grand Rapids
Holland
Lansing (2)
Northville
South Lyon
Okemos
Traverse City
Trenton

MINNESOTA
Burnsville
Duluth (2)
Minneapolis
Minnetonka
St. Paul
Waite Park

MISSISSIPPI
Jackson

MISSOURI
Independence
Kirkwood
Chesterfield
St. Peters
St. Louis

MONTANA
Billings
Bozeman
Butte
Great Falls
Missoula
Whitefish

NEBRASKA
Omaha (2)

NEVADA
Henderson
Las Vegas
Reno

NEW JERSEY
Cherry Hill

NEW MEXICO
Albuquerque (2)

NEW YORK
Buffalo

NORTH CAROLINA
Chapel Hill
Fayetteville
Greensboro
Wilmington

NORTH DAKOTA
Fargo

OHIO
Boardman

Findlay
Mentor
Stow
Sylvania
Upper Arlington
Westerville

OREGON
Bend
Clackamas
Corvallis
Eugene
Hillsboro
Medford
Portland
Salem (2)

PENNSYLVANIA
Pittsburgh
Wayne

TENNESSEE
Chattanooga (2)
Germantown
Memphis
Nashville
Franklin

TEXAS
Arlington
Austin (2)
Dallas
Richardson
Houston (2)
Lubbock (2)
San Antonio
The Woodlands

UTAH
Bountiful
Layton
Logan
Ogden (2)
Orem
American Fork
Provo
Salt Lake City (2)
St. George
Taylorsville

VIRGINIA
Alexandria
Centreville
Herndon
Vienna

WASHINGTON
Ballard
Bellevue
Bellingham
Federal Way
Redmond
Seattle (2)
Spokane (2)
Tacoma

WISCONSIN
De Pere
Eau Claire
Elm Grove
Greendale
Madison
Neenah
Whitefish Bay